BEHIND THE SCENES AT THE
ZOO

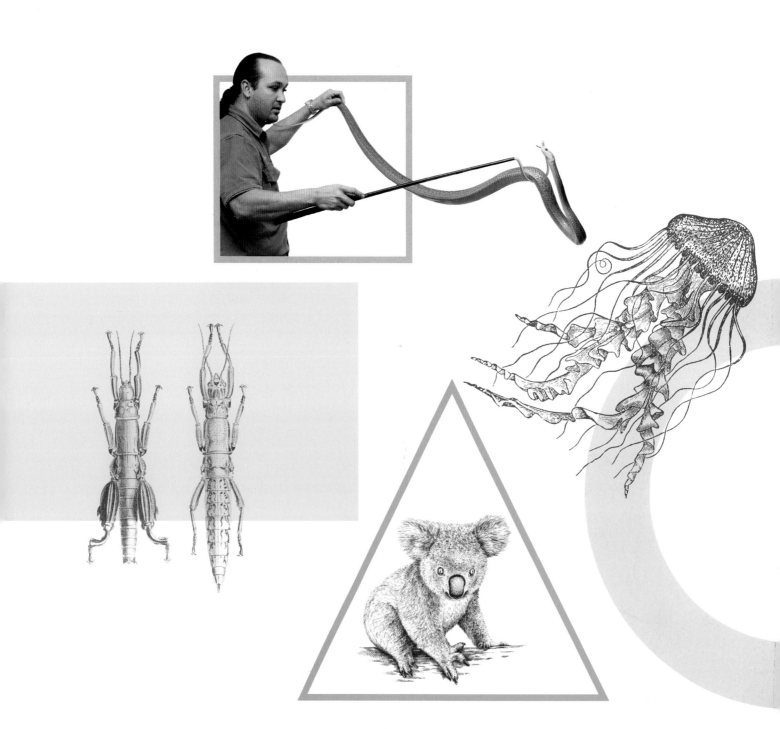

BEHIND THE SCENES
AT THE
ZOO

YOUR ALL-ACCESS GUIDE TO THE
WORLD'S GREATEST ZOOS AND AQUARIUMS

Consultant Vicky Melfi

Senior Editor Pauline Savage
Senior Designer Smiljka Surla
Assistant Editor Tayabah Khan
US Editor Jennette ElNaggar
Designer Anna Pond
Design Assistant Lauren Quinn
Writers Ben Ffrancon Davies, Vicky Melfi
Picture Researcher Laura Barwick

Managing Editor Rachel Fox
Managing Art Editor Owen Peyton Jones
Production Editor George Nimmo
Senior Production Controller Meskerem Berhane
Jacket Designers Akiko Kato, Tanya Mehrotra
DTP Designer Rakesh Kumar
Jackets Design Development Manager Sophia MTT

Publisher Andrew Macintyre
Art Director Karen Self
Associate Publishing Director Liz Wheeler
Publishing Director Jonathan Metcalf

First American Edition, 2021
Published in the United States by DK Publishing
1450 Broadway, Suite 801, New York, NY 10018

A catalog record for this book
is available from the Library of Congress.
ISBN 978-0-7440-2888-1

DK books are available at special discounts when purchased
in bulk for sales promotions, premiums, fund-raising, or educational use.
For details, contact: DK Publishing Special Markets,
1450 Broadway, Suite 801, New York, NY 10018
SpecialSales@dk.com

Printed and bound in China

For the curious
www.dk.com

MIX
Paper from
responsible sources
FSC™ C018179

This book was made with Forest Stewardship Council ™ certified
paper—one small step in DK's commitment to a sustainable future.

For more information go to www.dk.com/our-green-pledge

CONTENTS

3

4

THE WORLD OF ZOOS

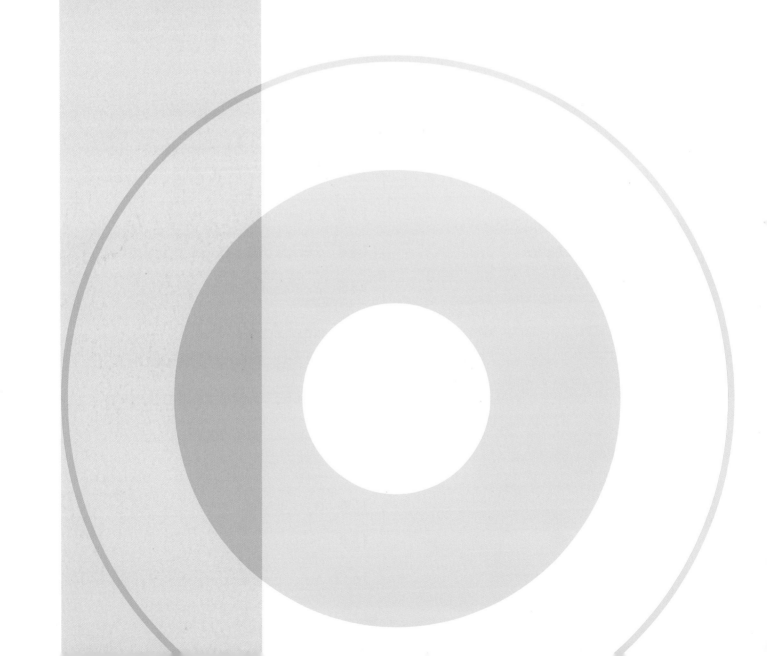

Welcome to the wonderful world of zoos! Earth is home to an abundance of wildlife, and zoos bring some of this incredible biodiversity together so that you can enjoy seeing amazing animals, plants, and habitats from every corner of the planet—things that you might never otherwise come across. The money you pay to visit supports the care of the animals in the zoo and—just as important—goes toward research and conservation programs that happen far beyond the zoo's gates. Running a zoo requires people with different skills and specialties. Together, this dedicated army of keepers, conservationists, and researchers works toward a common goal: to shape a healthy planet, for wildlife and for humankind.

WHAT IS A ZOO?

Zoos are collections of animals that you can pay to see. They include aquariums, which house animals that live in water, and wildlife or safari parks, which you can often drive through. Most zoo visitors come to have a great day out, like those watching the giant panda here at River Safari in Singapore. Zoos hope their visitors will be inspired by the animals they see and discover what they can do to save them from extinction—zoos are home to some of Earth's most endangered species.

A careful balancing act

Educating visitors about animals and the threats they face is the key focus for many zoos, such as Amnéville Zoo in France, where audiences are taught about the wonder of sea lions. While you can see the animals, they can see you, too, so zoos have to get the balance right to ensure zoo visitors don't cause any distress.

TYPES OF ZOOS

No two zoos are the same, but what all zoos have in common is a passion for conservation and a desire to look after their animals in the best way possible. How they do this depends on where they are, how much space they have, and the kinds of animals they house.

CITY ZOOS

Situated in busy city centers, city zoos are an oasis of nature in the middle of bustling urban surroundings. Some of the most famous zoos in the world are based in cities, such as Berlin Zoo in Germany and Beijing Zoo in China. Their location in tourist hot spots helps city zoos attract a lot of visitors, and the money from these ticket sales is channeled back into animal care, research, and conservation.

Honolulu Zoo in the US

WILDLIFE PARKS

Wildlife parks, also called safari parks, offer a more immersive experience than city zoos. As well as being a lot bigger, many of them have habitat zones that visitors can drive through to see the animals. Their size means that they are based in the countryside, but some wildlife parks are paired with city zoos, such as Highland Wildlife Park and Edinburgh Zoo in the UK.

Woburn Safari Park in the UK

SPECIALIST ZOOS

Many zoos are home to a huge variety of animals, but others prefer to focus their attention on one particular group, such as reptiles or butterflies. By concentrating on a smaller number of species, these zoos can offer specialized care and can target their conservation and research efforts, too.

Jurong Bird Park in Singapore

AQUARIUMS

Aquariums are home to animals and plants that thrive in and near water. Most are situated by large rivers or the sea, to allow them access to the water they need for their tanks. They often feature glass tunnels and walkways to give visitors a great view of this underwater world. Some larger zoos may have an aquarium as one of their many exhibits, whereas other aquariums are stand-alone attractions in their own right.

The Oceanographic in Spain

OTHER TYPES OF ZOOS

Zoos go by many names. Here are two more of them:

▶ BIOPARKS

A combination of zoo and botanic garden (where collections of plants are viewed, studied, and conserved), bioparks showcase how plants and animals coexist in healthy habitats. Also called ecoparks, they highlight the value of biodiversity—the variety of all life on Earth—and often allow animals to roam freely, using natural barriers such as moats to separate them from visitors if necessary.

▶ CHILDREN'S ZOOS

These zoos give young children a chance to learn about animals in a way that suits their age—the zoos themselves are smaller and tend to house smaller animals, too. Those called "farm parks" or "petting zoos" allow children to touch or help feed and groom farmyard and domestic animals.

DID YOU
KNOW?

Many of London Zoo's buildings, including a traditional telephone box, are important and need to be preserved.

Ancient collections

This ancient Egyptian wall painting from c. 1425 BCE shows Nubian people bringing long-horned cattle, giraffes, panthers, elephants, and monkeys as tributes to the powerful Egyptian nobleman Rekhmire. Private animal collections like these became symbols of status and wealth.

THE HISTORY OF ZOOS

People around the world have kept wild animals in captivity for thousands of years. Often, animals were offered as gifts between kings, queens, and other powerful people. These collections of animals later became known as "menageries." What we now think of as zoos began during the 18th and 19th centuries, when visitors were invited in to look at and learn about animals.

◀ Open to the public

In 1828, the Zoological Society of London established London Zoo for scientists to study animals. It opened to the general public in 1847. People were excited to see for the first time many "exotic" animals (animals from other parts of the world) they never knew existed.

Zoos in the 20th century

Zoos soon became a popular day out. Enclosures of the time often featured heavy metal bars. In the 1930s, a child visiting Dublin Zoo in Ireland still managed to feed the elephants, despite the additional barrier that was supposed to keep visitors and animals safe.

TODAY'S ZOOS

Zoos and aquariums today are organizations for animal conservation and welfare, which are areas they excel in. They encourage their visitors to be kind to the planet and to help save animals from extinction. They keep animals safe in captivity, breed them for release into the wild, protect and restore habitats, and help the communities living alongside wildlife. Behind the scenes, pioneering zoo researchers are making fascinating discoveries about animals. Zoos use this knowledge to look after animals in a way that maximizes their welfare. Today's zoos showcase their unique animal collections and, with their talented staff, inspire change for a better world.

▶ Happy animals

Zoos want their animals to be happy—but it's hard to know what happiness for an animal is. It's probably not just being healthy, long-lived, or having offspring, and more about choices—being able to decide to explore, play, or hide. These tigers at Cologne Zoo in Germany have plenty of opportunities to choose whether to drink, bathe, scratch fallen trees, or hide from each other or from visitors.

NOT ALL ZOOS ARE EQUAL

There are thousands of zoos in the world. So what makes a good one? Good zoos and aquariums are members of accreditation associations. To become a member, zoos have to show that they have high standards of animal care, contribute to conservation, actively educate their visitors, and conduct scientific research. Zoo associations also enable good zoos to work collaboratively and achieve more together than they could on their own.

ZOO DEPARTMENTS

It takes a lot of people to run a zoo! It's not surprising that zoos attract those who love animals and have a passion for conservation, but a successful zoo needs people with experience in all kinds of different things, from business to catering and horticulture to education. Some zoo staff work in other countries, supporting animals in the wild. Others work jointly with universities, conducting research.

ANIMAL MANAGEMENT

Zookeepers, curators, vets, and other staff make sure animals thrive at the zoo. Keepers are responsible for their daily welfare, like this keeper at Singapore Zoo, who is observing douc langurs prior to feeding them. Curators make decisions about the lives of animals, such as whether or not they might breed. Vets work to ensure that animals remain healthy.

CONSERVATION

Staff working in conservation might specialize in animals, habitats, people, or management. Successful projects combine work both in the zoo and in native habitats, caring for endangered species and the communities living alongside them. Saint Louis Zoo works with the Grevy's Zebra Trust in Kenya, whose local staff monitor zebra populations, regenerate habitats, and support local people.

EDUCATION

Zoos attract more than 700 million visitors worldwide every year. Raising awareness of the work zoos do, and showing how we can all change our behavior to benefit the planet, are the most powerful ways zoos can help save wildlife from extinction. Here at Munich's Hellabrunn Zoo in Germany, a science educator talks to a group of young people about animals, their biology, and the threats they face.

RESEARCH

Zoo scientists study animals in zoos and in the wild, using what they learn to improve conservation and the lives of captive animals. Their studies of animal behavior, health, and genetics have increased our understanding of animals and their needs. Reproductive biologists, such as the vet pictured here analyzing giant panda sperm at Beauval Zoo in France, have helped increase the numbers of endangered species through artificial reproduction.

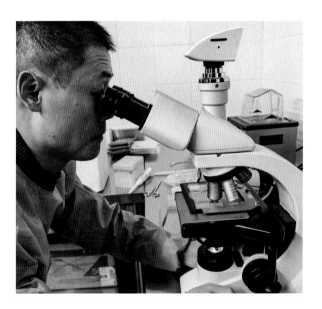

OTHER TEAMS

Other departments needed to make a zoo run smoothly include:

▶ NUTRITION
Nutritionists design diets for each species at the zoo, making adjustments according to the age of the animals and also if they're pregnant or nursing.

▶ MARKETING AND COMMUNICATIONS
Campaign managers and social media professionals raise awareness of a zoo's good work and highlight how human behavior is affecting the planet.

▶ MAINTENANCE
Different teams maintain the safety and comfort of animals, staff, and visitors by ensuring all parts of the zoo—from enclosures to signposts—are clean and in good condition.

▶ FINANCE
Zoos are businesses and need accountants to help them be financially secure.

THE WORLD OF ANIMALS

To make sense of the millions of different animal species, scientists have created groups based on their similarities. Every animal is defined as either a vertebrate (having a backbone inside its body) or an invertebrate (having no backbone). Animals can be further divided into six groups (called "classes"): mammals, insects, birds, amphibians, fish, and reptiles.

▶ Mammals

Mammals are warm-blooded animals that breathe air and have hair. They are found in every major habitat in the world—both on land and in water. The 5,000 or so mammal species vary in size from the tiniest mouse to the huge blue whale. Females generally give birth to live young and produce milk for them. Most are placentals, meaning they grow their baby inside their body using an organ called a placenta. There are two more types of mammals: marsupials and monotremes.

GREEN RINGTAIL POSSUM

Marsupials
Young marsupials are born underdeveloped and will continue to grow in their mother's pouch. Most marsupials, such as koalas and kangaroos, are found in Australasia, although some, such as the opossum, live in the Americas.

PLATYPUS

Monotremes
These unusual mammals lay eggs rather than give birth to live young. The five species of monotremes— the platypus and four types of echidna—are found only in Australia and Papua New Guinea.

As a male mandrill becomes more dominant in the group, its colorful markings become brighter and more attractive to females.

MANDRILL

▶ Insects

Insects are invertebrates, but they have an external skeleton (exoskeleton) that helps protect their bodies. An insect's body consists of three parts: a head, thorax, and abdomen. Insects come in a lot of shapes, from beetles to stick insects, but the thing that all insects have in common is that they always have six legs. They usually have two antennae, and most have wings, too.

LYCHEE SHIELD BUG

ANIMALS IN DANGER

Throughout this book, you'll read that animals are in other sorts of groups. The IUCN Red List of Threatened Species™ (see p.128) has assessed the threats to more than 125,000 species and given them a category that describes their risk of extinction. Animals in the categories of Vulnerable, Endangered, and Critically Endangered are considered to be threatened with extinction. Here are the categories explained:

Least Concern
Species that are currently considered to be safe from extinction

Near Threatened
Species that are likely to become threatened in the near future

Vulnerable
Species at high risk of extinction

Endangered
Species at very high risk of extinction

Critically Endangered
Species at extremely high risk of extinction

Extinct in the Wild
Species that exist only in captivity

Extinct
Species that no longer exist

EARTH'S WILDLIFE

Animals have evolved two different ways to control their temperature. Mammals and birds are warm-blooded and shiver to warm up and sweat to cool down. Amphibians, fish, and reptiles are cold-blooded—their temperature reflects their environment. To get warm, they might bask in the sun on a rock, and to cool themselves, they might seek shade underneath it.

▼ Birds

Birds can be seen as living dinosaurs, having evolved from the giant reptiles that once roamed Earth. They have two legs, a bill, and feathers, as well as hollow bones, which make their body light enough to overcome gravity and swoop through the skies. Not all birds can fly—penguins use their wings to propel themselves through the oceans instead.

KEEL-BILLED TOUCAN

A toucan's bill is made out of keratin—the same substance as human hair and nails.

▼ Amphibians

Most amphibians, from frogs to newts, start life as larvae in the water. They undergo a process called metamorphosis, in which they dramatically change into their adult form, and then live on land. Poisonous species have brightly colored skin to warn off predators.

DID YOU KNOW?

The fluorescent skin of the polka-dot tree frogs may help them see each other at night.

POLKA-DOT TREE FROG

◀ Fish

Fish are covered in scales, glide under the water using their tail and fins, and breathe using gills. From miniature guppies to gigantic whale sharks, fish are incredibly diverse. They are found in both saltwater and freshwater habitats and can live in warm tropical waters as well as icy ones.

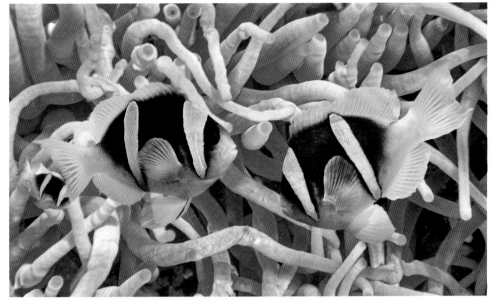

CLOWNFISH

Panther chameleons may change color to help regulate their temperature.

Chameleons' eyes can move independently of each other to look in different directions.

PANTHER CHAMELEON

▶ Reptiles

Covered in bony plates, scaly skin, or both, reptiles are found in all types of habitats. Some reptiles, such as geckos, live on land, whereas others, such as turtles, thrive under water. Every species breathes air—even aquatic reptiles come to the surface to gulp enough air for their next deep dive.

MAKING A ZOO

The best zoos today keep their animals in beautiful enclosures that meet their needs, allow staff to work safely, and give visitors a great experience. A lot of thought goes into making a zoo, whether it's being designed from scratch or having old enclosures updated. Then there's the question of filling these new spaces with animals—no zoo should take animals from the wild unless it's to protect them. Instead, zoos work together to manage the numbers of animals they have and to ensure they are saved from extinction.

LANDSCAPE
ARCHITECT

Designing zoos is the job of a landscape architect. Some zoos bring in outside experts, while others, such as the Smithsonian's National Zoo in the US, have their own in-house landscape architect. Architects first have to understand the needs of animals, visitors, and keepers. Then they are able to create stunning but practical enclosures that also give animals a safe and stimulating space to live and play.

Teamwork

Architects at the zoo design everything from enclosures to food stalls and walkways. They work with colleagues from all over the zoo to devise the perfect plans.

From concept to creation ▲
This in-house landscape architect at the Smithsonian's National Zoo has had the chance to see her paper plans transformed into a real-life enclosure.

Using technology

Many ideas start as sketches on paper, but to create the real deal, landscape architects use design software. These complex computer programs ensure every plan is perfectly precise so that the build goes off without a hitch.

DESIGNING A ZOO

With animals, visitors, and staff to consider, planning a zoo is a complex business. When Chester Zoo in the UK wanted a new area, they decided to base it on six islands of south-east Asia. Called "Islands," the theme was carried through all aspects, from animal enclosures to food outlets, to create a wraparound experience for visitors that highlights the importance of conserving endangered species.

Education center
Visitors can learn about the unique south-east Asian animal and plant species found in the Islands exhibit and how the zoo is working to protect this wildlife.

Boat ride
A boat ride is a relaxing way to travel through the islands, giving people an alternative way to see remarkable animals up close.

Enclosures
Creating a new area from scratch allowed the zoo to custom-build enclosures, like the cassowary exhibit, that meet the individual needs of each animal species.

Restaurant
All that island exploring can make people hungry, so an on-site restaurant serves up authentic Indonesian street food to complete the experience.

Shop
The gift shop lets guests pick up a souvenir of their fun day out, and the money raised by these sales is put toward the zoo's conservation projects.

Monsoon forest
Architects got creative with this real-life indoor rain forest, home to hundreds of animals and plants. Birds fly around above, and sometimes it even "rains" inside the building!

Conservation clues
Dotted around the exhibit are little huts filled with objects left by conservationists. It's a great way to educate visitors about the issues animals face in the wild.

HOUSING ANIMALS

Every animal at the zoo needs the right sort of home, called an enclosure or exhibit. Enclosures should meet the unique needs of each species and enable zoo staff to do their job efficiently and safely. Through signs and information boards, they should tell a bigger story to visitors about the animals they see: the wild places where they can be found across the world, and the ways in which people can support their conservation. Many zoos are aware of climate issues and try to design environmentally friendly places to keep their animals.

▶ Under one roof

The Equatorial Dome in France's Beauval Zoo is home to around 200 species, including aquatic Caribbean manatees, land-dwelling Komodo dragons, and tree-living squirrel monkeys. Because each species lives in a specific area of the exhibit, the animals are able to peacefully coexist together.

Safety first

The barriers in zoos keep animals, visitors, and zoo staff safe. Frankfurt Zoo in Germany separates its aardvark from the public using a glass window, which still allows them a good view. It's important that people don't bang on the glass when looking at animals!

Room to roam

Space for enclosures is limited in many zoos, so providing animals with opportunities to see the world around them can be a challenge. The tigers at Philadelphia Zoo have aerial walkways that allow them to roam and get a good look at other parts of the zoo.

Allowing natural behaviors

Enclosures should enable animals to perform their natural behaviors. Some species like to be in large groups; others are solitary animals. This snow leopard at Marwell Zoo in the UK has a lot of rocks and narrow ledges so that it can practice its climbing and balancing skills.

Keeping everyone happy

When visitors can really see the animals, they are more interested in them and their conservation. Some animals don't like visitors to get too close. Lookout towers at Auckland Zoo in New Zealand give people a fantastic view over this mixed-species enclosure—from a distance.

ELEPHANT HOUSE

The Kaeng Krachan Elephant Park at Zürich Zoo in Switzerland is home to a family of Asian elephants. At its center is the huge elephant house, with a beautiful roof made of wood. The exhibit includes unique design features tailored to meet the needs of the elephants—for example, they walk on a floor of sand, which helps keep their feet healthy. Elephants love to bathe, and the zoo has made sure that visitors can get a good view of these giants under water.

Learning about elephants
Visitors view the elephants from walkways within the enclosure. They also learn about elephant conservation and the zoo's efforts to support people and elephants living together in Thailand.

Outside space

Elephants can move between the inside and outside areas of the enclosure so that they can choose how close (or not) they want to be to their relatives.

Light and shade
Wild elephant behavior follows a daily rhythm, responding to changes in the amount of light. The skylights and wooden struts ensure plenty of light and shade.

Planting
Trees and vegetation create a natural environment but are protected from the elephants, which would destroy them. The elephants' food is grown elsewhere.

Off for a dip
Elephants are good swimmers. The elephant park has six pools, some of them deep, so the elephants get plenty of exercise.

AWESOME ENCLOSURES

Zoos want their animals to thrive, and the best way to make that happen is to carefully recreate their native habitats, whether that's a steamy African jungle or the icy Arctic. The main aim is to provide a safe and stimulating home for the animals, while also giving visitors a great experience. Some zoos have gotten truly creative with their enclosures and have won awards for their designs.

"ZOO IMMERSION"

At Fuengirola Biopark in Spain, all the habitats are designed to fully immerse visitors in ecosystems from Madagascar to southeast Asia and the Pacific islands. Even the safety barriers are created using natural features such as rivers, rock walls, or fallen tree trunks.

The Bornean gibbon is one of the several endangered species on view.

SCHMUTZER PRIMATE CENTRE

Based at Rangunan Zoo in Jakarta, Indonesia, this fantastic conservation center houses many rare primates from around the world. A viewing platform lets you peer into the western lowland gorillas' wild-forest habitat. Elsewhere, a tunnel takes you through a natural tropical rain forest where the orangutans live.

POLAR FRONTIER

At Columbus Zoo and Aquarium, the polar bears' pool has a tidal machine that mimics their natural ocean habitat. A glass tunnel lets you surround yourself in the bears' underwater world.

167,000

The number of gallons of water in the main pool

BURGERS' BUSH

Burgers' Zoo in the Netherlands has created its very own tropical rain forest, with plants and animals from Africa, Asia, and the Americas. Sprinklers spray 21,000 gallons (80,000 liters) of water over the habitat, known as Burgers' Bush, to recreate the natural humidity of these forests.

1,000

The number of plant species in Burgers' Bush

PANGOLIN DOME

This dome structure in Taipei Zoo is modeled on the shape of a Formosan pangolin, a subspecies of the Critically Endangered Chinese pangolin found on the island. Designed to raise awareness, the dome houses a habitat based on the Amazon rain forest.

There are eight species of pangolins. Four species are found in Asia, while four species are native to Africa.

NATURAL ENCLOSURES

Salzburg Zoo in Austria has combined the surrounding mountainous landscape into the zoo's own architecture, building enclosures along the cliff face. Griffin vultures live around the zoo, nesting in the nearby mountains. The zoo even feeds them, and visitors can see the vultures swooping into the zoo for something to eat.

MORE TO SEE

▶ SUMATRAN ORANGUTAN EXHIBIT

Perth Zoo in Australia decided not to plant real trees in its rain forest enclosure, as the superstrong orangutans might quickly destroy them. Instead, the zoo created a "steel forest" climbing frame of metal branches and ropes for the orangutans to climb.

▶ PONGOLAND

The ape enclosure at Leipzig Zoo in Germany is built to resemble a real jungle. Even the walls of the enclosure look like embankments and rock. Visitors can walk through the exhibit, separated from the animals by natural barriers such as lakes and streams.

INSIDE AREAS

Many animal exhibits have both outside and inside areas. Outside areas are usually larger and naturalistic, offering animals plenty of opportunities to show off various behaviors for the watching visitors. Inside areas usually allow keepers a good view of the animals. Here, keepers provide animals with food, shelter, and anything else they need.

▶ Learning about each other

The inside areas of exhibits are often smaller than those outside, like here at Paris Zoo in France. While visitors can view the animals through glass windows up above, the inside enclosure is where the zookeepers and the animals get to know each other. Giraffes can be shy, so another window lets them get used to the keepers and their daily duties. At the same time, keepers learn the needs and preferences of each giraffe.

Getting up and out

During the day, these dama gazelles at the Smithsonian's National Zoo share an exhibit with Rüppell's griffon vultures and scimitar-horned oryx. They spend the night in separate indoor pens and walk back to their shared enclosure in the morning.

AQUARIUM UPKEEP

Have you ever thought about the water in an aquarium? Fish need clean water just like we need clean air. A lot of work goes into keeping tanks in tip-top condition to maintain the perfect ecosystem for all an aquarium's aquatic inhabitants. There are complex systems that filter the water, keeping it free from toxic bacteria and chemicals but rich in oxygen.

▶ Keeping it clean

Many steps are taken to make sure the water is clean before it reaches the tank, but the tank itself and some of its inhabitants need a scrub from time to time, too. While cleaning the inside of this aquarium tank, an aquarist (trained to care for marine and freshwater life) at Lisbon Oceanarium in Portugal brushes up some coral to keep it clean and healthy.

Testing the water

Aquarium staff regularly test the pH level of the water in each of their tanks to make sure that it is just right for the animals that live in it. If the water is too acidic or too alkaline, they quickly rebalance it.

Life support system

The aquarium at uShaka Sea World in South Africa uses 470 pumps and a 14-mile (22 km) network of pipes to collect seawater for its underwater exhibits.

Natural filtration
Pipes at the end of this specially built pier collect seawater for the aquarium. As it's drawn up through the sand, the water goes through a natural filtration process.

Pumped up
To make the water super safe for the aquarium exhibits, it goes through biological filters, protein skimmers, and another sand filter. A chilling system keeps the temperature just right.

AMAZING AQUARIUMS

Aquariums give you a fish's-eye view of the deepest reaches of the oceans. You get a chance to see creatures that are normally hidden in their underwater world, and researchers are able to study them to help and encourage conservation efforts. This is especially important in the fight against plastic pollution, which threatens some of the oceans' most endangered species.

DUBAI AQUARIUM AND UNDERWATER ZOO

This huge aquarium is, unusually, located in a shopping center and is home to more than 140 species of aquatic animals. You can also walk through a 115 ft (48 m) tunnel set deep under water.

2,640,000
The number of gallons in the main tank

GEORGIA AQUARIUM

The largest aquarium in the US, and the third-largest in the world, Georgia Aquarium is home to a huge range of marine life, including beluga whales, American alligators, and great hammerhead sharks. Thousands of school children go every year to learn about aquatic ecosystems.

One of the aquarium's biggest attractions, an adult purple-striped jellyfish's bell can be up to 3 ft (1 m) wide.

S.E.A. AQUARIUM

South East Asia Aquarium in Singapore is the second-largest aquarium in the world. It features an enormous viewing screen and a tunnel walkway.

Graceful manta rays swim in one of 45 different marine habitats.

AQUAMARINE FUKUSHIMA

This marine science museum in Japan specializes in the study of fossils and "living fossils"—animals that have been almost unchanged by evolution for hundreds of thousands of years. It has a unique triangular tunnel that runs between its recreation of the two ocean currents that collide to the east of Japan.

TWO OCEANS AQUARIUM

This aquarium in South Africa gets its name from its location at the southern tip of the African continent, where the Indian and Atlantic oceans meet. The kelp forest exhibit, where native fish swim through giant sea bamboo and algae fronds, is one of only a handful in the world. The tank is open to the sky so that the plants receive sunlight for photosynthesis.

ATLANTIC SEA-PARK

This aquarium on the stunning coastline near Ålesund in Norway tells visitors about Norwegian marine life, with outdoor exhibits such as Seal Bay (Europe's largest seal enclosure) that show animals in their natural environments.

One tank is devoted to herring, a very important food source for Norwegian people.

MORE TO SEE

▶ **THE OCEANOGRAPHIC**
In a building designed to look like waves, this coastal aquarium in Valencia in Spain has Europe's longest underwater tunnel, which visitors can walk through as sharks circle above.

▶ **LISBON OCEANARIUM**
At this Portuguese aquarium, four marine habitats surround a large central tank, creating the illusion of a single ocean scene. This brings together land and sea ecosystems from all around the world.

▶ **VANCOUVER AQUARIUM**
More than 70,000 creatures live at this Canadian aquarium and marine research center, which focuses on keeping pollution out of Earth's oceans.

CAPTIVE BREEDING

Zoos manage their animals so that their populations can maintain themselves—it's crucial that animals aren't taken from the wild to fill a zoo. Zoos use a studbook, which contains information about zoo animals, to decide which animals to breed, a process known as "captive breeding." Sometimes, animals are exchanged between zoos to avoid inbreeding.

The mother carries her young babies around on her back.

Safety populations

Captive breeding ensures the survival of a species, even if it becomes extinct in the wild. Bristol Zoo in the UK bred a "safety population" of Critically Endangered Desertas wolf spiders. This species is endemic to Deserta Grande, a Portuguese island in the Atlantic Ocean, and could be wiped out by just one natural disaster.

▼ A healthy balance

Zoo populations need to be carefully managed. If there are too many babies, zoos will use contraception or separate the males and females to prevent any more births for a while. When these cubs from Germany's Hagenbeck Zoo are older, the males may move to another zoo to start their own pride.

In the wild, female lions are the primary hunters in the group.

PARTHENOGENESIS

Some female animals can breed all by themselves. In a process called "parthenogenesis," the eggs of the Komodo dragon, ball python, and some fish, birds, and insects, can develop without fertilization by a male. Depending on the species, the young that hatch are either full clones or half-clones of their mother.

Natural breeding

When looking to breed animals, keepers try to let them interact and pair off naturally. Keepers at Gaia Zoo in the Netherlands are introducing these hamsters to each other in the hope that they will want to mate.

This female's muscles shiver to keep her eggs warm until they hatch.

A male lion's mane gives a female information about his health and fighting skills.

DID YOU

KNOW?

The Arabian oryx was Extinct in the Wild. It was reintroduced to the Arabian Peninsula after a captive breeding program.

BALL PYTHON

There are usually two or three cubs per litter.

LORD HOWE ISLAND STICK INSECT

This species of stick insect was once thought to be extinct—wiped out by black rats that invaded Lord Howe Island, located east of mainland Australia, after a shipwreck in 1918. But in 2001, a tiny population of Lord Howe Island stick insects was discovered by chance on a nearby island. Two pairs were taken to Melbourne Zoo in Australia, and a breeding program was launched. Other zoos have since started breeding the insects to bring this precious animal back from the brink of extinction, and several thousand now exist in captivity—although to this day, there are thought to be only 24 individuasls left in the wild.

▶ Successful start

Adult insects and eggs have been sent to other zoos in Australia and overseas to create safety populations of this Critically Endangered species. When these stick insects laid eggs at Bristol Zoo in the UK, it was the first time this had ever happened outside of Australia.

From egg to nymph

To stand a chance of saving what is often called the world's rarest insect, zoos have had to understand how they breed. Males and females mate to produce offspring, although the females are also capable of parthenogenesis (reproduction without the help of a male), where unfertilized eggs develop into clones of the mother.

The female lays 10 eggs at a time. Once the eggs have been laid, she covers them with soil to hide and protect them.

The little beige eggs are only about ⅕ in (½ cm) long and are covered with a raised pattern. A female can lay 300 in her lifetime.

After about 26 weeks, the eggs hatch. A newly hatched nymph (the juvenile form) is much larger than its egg.

The stick insect gets darker with each exoskeleton it sheds.

DID YOU

KNOW?

Lord Howe Island stick insects are also known as "tree lobsters" due to their large size and shape.

The hatchling's bright green coloring helps it to blend in with its leafy environment. It becomes darker as it grows older.

Melaleuca leaves

In the wild, Lord Howe Island stick insects feed mainly on leaves from the Melaleuca tree—commonly known as the tea tree. In zoos they may be fed on a wider variety of plants.

ON THE MOVE

Zoos try to avoid moving animals whenever possible, but there are times when it's necessary. It may be to take part in a breeding program with animals in another zoo or a short trip to see a specialist vet or even a permanent move to a new home. Keepers take every precaution when moving animals to keep them comfortable and to minimize stress.

▶ Out and about

This young giraffe is on its way from Taronga Western Plains Zoo in Dubbo, Australia, to Taronga Zoo in Sydney—a 250 mile (400 km) journey. It's being transported in a specially built container, offering it plenty of fresh air and the opportunity to see out while on the road.

Arriving by plane

For the journey from the Philippine Eagle Foundation in the Philippines to the Jurong Bird Park in Singapore, two Critically Endangered Philippine eagles traveled in a temperature-controlled section of the plane's hold, and each had a separate crate.

Safe arrival
The crates, with plenty of holes for ventilation, have kept the eagles safe and comfortable during the trip. Detailed labels let the crew know to treat them with the utmost care.

Checking it over
Once each eagle is off the plane, keepers carry out a quick health check. The bird is wearing a mask that covers its eyes to help it keep calm.

A new home

This hippopotamus has just arrived at Beauval Zoo in France. Keepers open the doors of the transportation crate and then take a step back, letting the hippo come out in its own time to explore its new surroundings.

3

CARING FOR ANIMALS

Animals in zoos need looking after every day, come rain or shine. Whether it's mucking out the enclosures or preparing mountains of fresh food, the life of the keepers is a busy one! It's important that keepers really know their animals, so they spend a lot of time observing them, measuring how they grow, and enabling them to behave as they would in the wild. There's always a vet on hand to ensure that animals are as healthy as possible. A cause for celebration in zoos is when a new animal is born—these often help boost the populations of endangered species.

ROLES BEHIND THE SCENES
ZOOKEEPER

Zookeepers work with—and get to know—some of the most interesting and exciting animals on the planet. They do much more than clean enclosures and feed animals—they have to be experts in all aspects of an animal's welfare. Zookeepers keep a close eye on an animal's physical and mental health and use their specialist knowledge to learn about each animal's personality. Some keepers will care for an animal throughout its entire life.

Someone familiar

For many zoo animals, keepers are a familiar and reassuring part of their life. At the Singapore Night Safari, a keeper helps a young Malayan tapir to settle after it's moved to a new enclosure.

▲ **Spot the difference**
This family of scarlet macaws at Paradise Park in the UK may all look the same to you, but the keeper knows each one by sight.

This educator explains to visitors why the lions are being trained.

Two keepers are training an adult female lion and her litter. Training helps the keepers monitor the lions' health.

Keeper talks

At Columbus Zoo and Aquarium, visitors learn about animals during one of the zoo's many keeper talks. These talks are a chance for zoo professionals to speak about their passion for animals and a great way for them to explain to visitors their zoo's mission: the conservation of endangered species.

Female gorillas in zoos first become pregnant when they are 8–10 years old.

▼ Looking after mom

Social animals, such as gorillas, will be looked after by the others in their group. Zoos just make sure that the mother-to-be stays healthy and calm and also has a place to go when she needs privacy. However, when the baby gorilla is born, everyone will want a look—when the mother allows!

Ultrasound scans
Vets perform scans on pregnant mammals to check that the baby is growing as expected and to identify any potential problems. Gorillas become pregnant only once every four years, so zoos try to learn as much as they can.

A gorilla's knuckles sometimes swell while she is pregnant.

Gorilla pregnancies last about eight and a half months.

BECOMING PARENTS

Animal pregnancies can last from just 12 days to more than 21 months, and one species can have vastly different needs from another during pregnancy. From regular health checks to giving vitamin supplements, keepers do their best to make sure that every pregnancy goes well. There's great excitement as the due date nears—most births occur at night, and some keepers like to stick around after hours to witness these rare events.

Nest rings

Keepers at Edinburgh Zoo in the UK have set out these nest rings along with a supply of pebbles for their gentoo penguins. After they've mated, the penguin pairs use the pebbles to make nests in the rings, where both the males and the females will look after the egg until it hatches.

Pebble proposal

When a male gentoo penguin finds a prospective mate, he "proposes" with the smoothest, shiniest pebble.

Male "mothers"

Although not quite the same as when a female is pregnant, in some unusual cases, the male carries the unborn young until they're ready to hatch.

Seahorse

When seahorses mate, the female leaves as many as 2,000 eggs in the male's brooding pouch, where he fertilizes them. He then carries them until they're ready to be released.

Yellow-headed jawfish

The male yellow-headed jawfish keeps a clutch of fertilized eggs in his mouth until they're ready to hatch, which is about nine days after fertilization. This process is known as "mouthbrooding."

54

The mother licks the calf to clean it.

A newborn giraffe's horns start out flat, but they'll stand up straight after just a few hours.

◀ A long drop

Giraffes give birth standing up, and the calf falls about 5 ft (1.5 m). Newborns are well adapted to survive this tumble, but zookeepers at Aalborg Zoo in Denmark have added extra hay to the enclosure to make doubly sure the new arrival doesn't get hurt. Giraffes are pregnant for 15 months, longer than almost any other animal, so the calves arrive very well developed. Taking only half an hour to stand up, the calf is even able to walk by the time it's an hour old.

Kangaroos can provide two different types of milk: one for the newborn and one for the older joey.

ANIMAL BIRTHS

All births at the zoo are eagerly awaited. When new arrivals are on the way, keepers try not to interfere, but they will lend a helping hand if the mother is struggling or if the newborn needs extra care. They often monitor a birth via CCTV to keep an eye out for any problems, and they may step in to make sure the mother stays safe and the babies arrive healthy.

DID YOU KNOW?

A kangaroo's pouch is called a "marsupium."

Marsupial births

Kangaroos give birth to live young, but, as marsupials, these tiny babies (called joeys) still have a lot more growing to do. After it's born, the joey crawls into its mother's pouch where it continues to grow. At around six months, it starts to venture out, but it won't leave for good for a few more months. A kangaroo can carry a newborn and an older joey in her pouch at the same time.

Latching on

Newborn joeys are born blind, deaf, and only ³⁄₁₆–1 in (5–25 mm) long. Climbing into the external pouch, they latch on to a nipple and suckle for about two months, developing there instead of in the uterus.

AALBORG ZOO

Opening in 1935, Aalborg Zoo in Denmark now has about 2,300 animals from 125 different species. The zoo plays a key part in a national effort to save the native population of wild barn owls, whose numbers have drastically reduced over the last few decades.

MANATEE MOTHER

This manatee from Beauval Zoo in France is part of a European breeding program and has just given birth to a calf. Manatees are classed as Vulnerable in the wild, so each birth helps to ensure the survival of the species. Like other aquatic mammals, manatees breathe oxygen from the air, but since a calf can't swim by itself until an hour after birth, it needs its mother's help to reach the surface to take its first breath.

Making observations

The pair need time to bond, so keepers keep their distance while watching over them. They'll usually wait a few days before carrying out essential health checks.

BEAUVAL ZOO

Opening in 1980 as a bird park, Beauval Zoo in France is home to nearly 35,000 animals from more than 800 species, including koalas, hyenas, and okapis. With many different habitats, such as the Elephant Plain and the Equatorial Dome, the zoo has stayed true to its roots with its Tropical Birds Greenhouse.

A NEW ARRIVAL

Any birth at the zoo is exciting, but the arrival of a giant panda cub, like this one at the Smithsonian's National Zoo, is particularly special. These rare animals are very difficult to breed—females are fertile for only two or three days a year. Although newborn cubs are tiny, weighing just 3½ oz (100 g), they quickly grow into strong and playful youngsters.

Panda cam

Like most newborns, giant panda cubs need constant care from their mothers. Keepers leave mother and baby alone, observing them from a live webcam. Cubs are born without their distinctive black-and-white markings, which appear at three weeks.

Playtime

Now that the male cub is four months old, the keepers introduce some enrichment. He seems to like playing with a red toy egg and an empty puzzle feeder, which help him learn to understand different kinds of objects.

CHEETAH CHECKUP

All newborns at the zoo are given a special
examination by the vet. Cheetah cubs have sharp
teeth and claws, so staff must follow strict rules
when handling these wild animals. Identifying any
medical issues early on helps zoos to provide the
best care to their cheetah cubs. The mother
herself will continue to look after her cubs until
they are 18 months old.

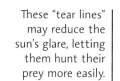

These "tear lines"
may reduce the
sun's glare, letting
them hunt their
prey more easily.

▶ Precious cubs

Cheetahs are classed as Vulnerable,
so births in a zoo contribute to
their conservation. Fewer than one
in 10 survive in the wild, but if all
goes well, these three will live for
12–15 years—around four or five
years longer than they would in
the wild—and will hopefully go on
to have cubs of their own.

Cheetah cubs have long hair along their back called a "mantle." It helps camouflage them when they are most vulnerable.

The vet examination

A vet at the Smithsonian Conservation Biology Institute in the US checks the health of this young cheetah cub. Of all the wild cat species, cheetahs have the smallest teeth, but they can still give the vet a nasty nip. Zookeepers help by holding the cub firmly, wearing thick gloves to prevent injury. Working quickly so the cub doesn't become stressed, everyone wears a mask to avoid passing on any human infections to the cub.

Cheetahs can't actually roar, but that doesn't stop this little cub from trying. The vet uses this opportunity to check the cub's teeth.

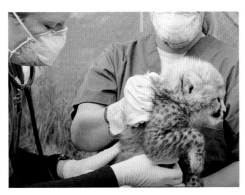

The vet starts her examination by using a stethoscope to listen to the cub's heart and lungs, to make sure these vital organs are working properly.

The cub is vaccinated against a variety of diseases. This is very important, as cheetahs are a lot more vulnerable to disease than many other mammals.

She uses an ophthalmoscope to check the cub's eyes. In the wild, cheetahs use their extraordinarily good eyesight to hunt prey as far as 3 miles (5 km) away.

After receiving some deworming medicine through a mouth syringe, it's good news for the cub—it's strong, healthy, and protected!

VITAL STATISTICS

Weighing and measuring animals regularly while they are young helps zoos know whether babies are developing as they should and whether they may need more (or less!) food. But the bond between mother and baby is really important, so taking measurements of young animals needs to be done sensitively, ideally without disturbing the family group.

▶ Standing tall

Zookeepers at Hagenbeck Zoo in Germany have found an ingenious way to measure the height of this baby giraffe without having to go near it. They've hung some hay above a measuring stick so that when the adults wander over to feed, the infant naturally follows them, neatly lining itself up against the markings on the board.

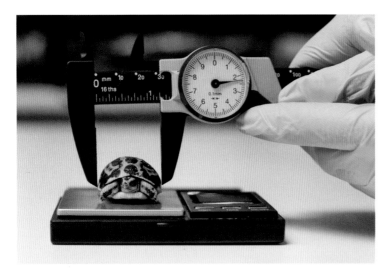

Baby scales

This baby Madagascan spider tortoise at Paignton Zoo in the UK is getting the full works. The width of a tortoise's shell is a good indicator of healthy growth, and these callipers are able to measure this tiny animal very precisely—even fully grown adults are only 6 in (15 cm) long. This tortoise seems happy to sit on these small scales while its weight is calculated at the same time.

HAGENBECK ZOO

Situated in Hamburg in Germany, Hagenbeck Zoo opened in 1907, at a time when using moats instead of barriers was very unusual. Building on this innovation, the zoo now includes a walk-through tropical aquarium and a polar sea exhibit to give its visitors an immersive experience as they visit more than 1,800 animals at the zoo.

Preparing a feast

Zoo nutritionists make diet plans for the species at the zoo. With so many different diets, they need to know what to feed insectivores, carnivores, and those animals that seem to eat everything—omnivores. Together with keepers, nutritionists plan diets that include fruits and vegetables, insects, meat, hay, and even bits of tree!

Chopping it up

This keeper at Berlin Zoo in Germany is busy slicing and dicing fruit and vegetables for the zoo's many animals. A lot of food is processed in these kitchens, as most animals need to be fed at least once a day. Almost 110 lb (50 kg) of vegetables need to be prepared—and that's just for the gorillas.

Diet plans

At the Smithsonian's National Zoo, keepers make up portions in plastic containers, following the diet plan book. Then they weigh it to check that the portion is the correct size. This ensures that each animal gets the nutrition it needs and maintains a healthy weight.

Brightly colored foods grab the tortoises' attention because they can see them easily.

Instead of teeth, they use their sharp beak for eating.

They push up with their powerful front legs to reach the food.

FEEDING HERBIVORES

When it comes to caring for animals, getting their diet right is one of the top priorities for a zoo. Herbivores (animals that eat plants, fruit, and vegetables) come in all shapes and sizes, and it's up to staff to plan and prepare meals so that each species receives the right sort of food to munch on—they'll even take into account the likes and dislikes of each individual. Keepers also come up with inventive ways to present food so that animals can use all their natural skills.

◀ Hungry tortoises

These Galápagos tortoises at London Zoo in the UK have been given hanging ropes of tasty vegetables. This unusual presentation of their daily diet stimulates the tortoises' minds as well as their appetites.

DID YOU KNOW?

Giant pandas at the Smithsonian's National Zoo chomp their way through 1,200 lb (545 kg) of bamboo every week.

FORAGING SKILLS

Feeding time at the zoo is more than just a mealtime. In the wild, animals have to look for their own food, known as "foraging". Keepers try to encourage an animal's natural foraging behavior and provide opportunities for them to find food in their enclosure.

▶ Hide and seek

By hiding food around this green iguana's enclosure, keepers at Paignton Zoo in the UK are helping it develop the food-gathering skills it would have learned in the wild. Iguanas are "folivores," meaning they mostly feed on leaves—although this one is enjoying a slice of red pepper!

Reaching up

Some herbivores, like these elephants at Prague Zoo in the Czech Republic, are given hay—cut and dried grass, legumes, or other plants. This is hung up high, so the elephants have to reach to eat it, just like they do when feeding on trees in the wild.

DID YOU
·
KNOW?

Tree-dwelling green
iguanas can change color
and can survive
a fall of 40-50 ft
(12-15 m).

WILD HABITS

As much as possible, zoos try to recreate the experiences an animal would have in the wild. With carnivorous animals, this means feeding them in a way that encourages their instinctive behavior—hunting and eating whole prey. Wild animals don't always eat every day, so zoos also follow this pattern, allowing a carcass to be eaten slowly over several days.

▶ Working as a pack

These African wild dogs at Sydney Zoo in Australia are devouring the carcass of a dead goat. This takes more time, effort, and energy than eating butchered meat, so it is good for their oral and digestive health. It also strengthens the bond between members of the pack.

Gnawing away

Zookeepers sometimes give carnivores bones instead of meat. At London Zoo in the UK, this has become a form of enrichment— keepers have tied up a bone so that the tiger has to search and reach for it.

CITY ZOOS

A city center is a surprisingly good spot for a zoo! Major cities are always full of tourists, and the zoos based there are big attractions in their own right. The huge amount of visitors means that zoos can raise awareness among a greater number of people about the threats animals face, and educate them about conservation.

THE NATIONAL ZOOLOGICAL GARDEN OF SOUTH AFRICA

Located in the middle of bustling Pretoria, South Africa's largest zoo is more commonly known as Pretoria Zoo. Dedicated to protecting South Africa's wildlife and biodiversity, the zoo is home to thousands of animals, such as this African wild dog, blue cranes, and green mambas.

The Critically Endangered Corroboree frog is part of Taronga Zoo's breeding program. Hundreds of these frogs have been released into the wild.

LONDON ZOO

The oldest scientific zoo in the world, London Zoo in the UK was first set up as a research center by the Zoological Society of London, but was opened to the public 19 years later. Full of firsts, London Zoo saw the world's first reptile house, insect house, and public aquarium.

1828

The year the zoo opened

TARONGA ZOO

Taronga Zoo in Sydney, Australia, aims to teach people that animals and humans can coexist and that it's everyone's responsibility to protect Earth's wildlife. The zoo focuses on conserving 10 rare and threatened species. Five species, including the platypus, are native to Australia, and five, including the Sunda pangolin, are from southeast Asia.

VIENNA ZOO

Dating back to 1752, this is the oldest zoo in the world and can be found in the heart of Vienna in Austria. This zoo started out as a small royal collection of animals but is now home to more than 700 species, such as Siberian tigers, penguins, and sea lions.

Vienna Zoo is located within the grounds of the Schönbrunn Palace.

SMITHSONIAN'S NATIONAL ZOO

Located in Washington, DC, the Smithsonian's National Zoo is a world-leading center for research and conservation. Among the animals here are American bison, one of the first species that the zoo set out to protect when it opened in 1887.

2,700
The number of animals at the zoo

SINGAPORE ZOO

Famous for its "open concept" idea, Singapore Zoo houses its animals, such as these hamadryas baboons, in areas that are very similar to their habitats in the wild. Not only does this open concept allow visitors to see the animals, such as fossas, leopards, and green basilisks, in a naturalistic setting, but it also helps keepers understand animal behavior. The zoo uses this information to help save endangered species.

MORE TO SEE

▶ **BEIJING ZOO**

This huge zoo is the oldest in China. Home to animals from all over the world, the zoo is well known for its work with rare animals endemic to China, such as giant pandas.

▶ **UENO ZOO**

Japan's oldest zoo has around 4,000 animals in its care, from slow lorises and pygmy hippos to Hokkaido brown bears and California sea lions.

▶ **DUBLIN ZOO**

Set up in 1831 as a private collection of mammals and birds, the zoo opened its doors to the public in 1840 and is now a big attraction in Ireland. It houses its animals in settings similar to their native habitats.

TRAINING ANIMALS

Animals learn all the time. They learn about their environment because they need to find food and shelter. They learn about other animals because they need to avoid predators. They also learn things in zoos, such as what time the keeper brings them food. Keepers sometimes decide to teach an animal a specific skill, for example, to sit or move on command. This type of learning is called training.

▶ Target training

Keepers use targets to show an animal where they want it to move in its enclosure or which part of its body to present for a health check. Different types of targets are used, depending on what best suits the animal's environment. At Florida Aquarium, a plastic orange disc is used to target this threatened Atlantic goliath grouper while it is measured.

Bells and whistles

Keepers can train an animal to respond to certain sounds (known as "auditory cues"). When this sea lion at Budapest Zoo in Hungary hears a whistle, it knows it should return to its keeper. Zookeepers also use bells and spoken commands to communicate with animals during training.

Hand signals

Animals are trained to take part in medical checks by recognizing hand signals. This orangutan at Singapore Zoo will open its mouth when it sees the keeper's index finger and thumb spread apart. Keepers can then check oral health on a regular basis in a way that minimizes animal stress.

Reinforcing behavior

When animals do something keepers want them to do, they get a treat. This is known as "reinforcing" behavior—it means the animal is more likely to do it again. At Paignton Zoo in the UK, a keeper gives the crocodile a hunk of meat after it moves to the target.

TARGET TRAINING IN ACTION

Training helps zookeepers provide animals with the care they need. At the Smithsonian's National Zoo, keepers have target trained two female Asian elephants to present different parts of their body to an orange ball attached to a stick. This simple technique enables keepers to move the animals around their enclosure safely and to take samples for health checks. Zookeepers sometimes carry out training sessions in which they show their visitors and new staff (those in red T-shirts) how they care for their elephants.

Foot inspection

Elephant feet carry a lot of weight—about six tons in fact! The tips of their digits are surrounded by a fatty pad similar to the heel of a human foot. At Blackpool Zoo in the UK, keepers train elephants to present their feet to be checked, to ensure their skin and nails are clean and uninjured.

DID YOU
KNOW?

An elephant has about 100,000 muscles, 40,000 of which are in its powerful trunk.

BIG CAT CARE

When caring for big cats, zoos use "protected contact." This means that keepers and animals never share the same space and are separated from each other by protective barriers. This poses a problem for things like medical checks—which is where target training comes in. At Germany's Hellabrunn Zoo, this tiger has been trained to touch the target. When the target moves, the tiger follows.

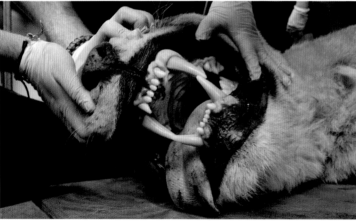

Dangerous dentistry

At Longleat safari park in the UK, a lion has been sedated for a medical procedure. Vets will use this time to check on its teeth as well. Good dental health is important in big cats, as they use their mouths not only to tear meat and gnaw bones but also to communicate with other lions and to move food or enrichment toys around their enclosure.

Careful contact

Using protected contact, keepers can monitor animals and carry out health checks safely. Strong wire mesh lets them get close, while the slight gaps allow for examinations and injections—and for the keeper to provide some small, tasty treats.

Close inspection
Preparing to do a mouth check, this lion and its keeper at Zagreb Zoo in Croatia are very close but separated from one another.

Showing a tail
Big cats at Hellabrunn Zoo in Germany are trained to present their tail through a gap under a secure barrier. The tail is the best place on a cat's body for a keeper to take a blood sample.

ENRICHMENT ACTIVITIES

Animals use a variety of behaviors to survive in the wild. They use their wonderfully different skills and bodies to find food, a mate, and a home. Zoos provide their animals with "enrichment"—activities or items that give each species an opportunity to make full use of their unique skills within the zoo environment.

▶ Learning new skills

Research has shown that octopuses are intelligent invertebrates. They have good memories, can solve problems, and can learn complex tasks. At Munich's Hellabrunn Zoo in Germany, the octopuses receive seafood in sealed jars. Using their strength and dexterity, they have to figure out how to open them.

Wild behavior

Animals in captivity are rarely able to use their hunting skills. At Paignton Zoo in the UK, keepers have provided this tiger with a wool and cardboard animal. The tiger gets to "hunt," handle new materials, and experience new smells.

FUN AND GAMES

Zookeepers use their understanding of how animals look at and move through the world so that they can provide them with the right sort of enrichment. They must consider which senses (sight, hearing, smell, taste, or touch) animals use and how they interact with their environment (with hands, hooves, or beaks) when creating enrichments for each species.

▶ A change of scene

Wild animals survive by adapting to changes in their environment. Letting zoo animals use their senses in new ways helps them develop survival skills. At Edinburgh Zoo in the UK, gentoo penguins get to see, feel, and taste bubbles.

Puzzle-feeder

When keepers hide some of an animal's daily food ration, the animal must use its own special skills to find it. At Singapore Zoo, a chimpanzee uses a tool (a stick) to access food from its puzzle-feeder.

Playtime

At Santa Fe College Teaching Zoo, an Asian small-clawed otter is playing with a soccer ball. Like many animals, it seems otters manipulate the objects they find to learn about them, gain food, and even just enjoy seeing them move around.

Food challenges

Sometimes, food can be given to animals in different ways so that they can experience new sensations and use different skills to eat it. At London Zoo in the UK, this squirrel monkey has to balance carefully to reach the fruit popsicles strung onto a rope.

New things to explore

Changing enclosure structures, like here at Reid Park Zoo, can provide animals with new places to explore or sleep. Some parts of the enclosure should remain unchanged and familiar, though, so that animals recognize that they're still home.

AQUARIST

Aquarists look after aquariums and the animals that live in them. They perform many different roles, such as cleaning tanks and checking the water quality—because fish live, eat, and poo in the same water, it's very important that the water is filtered and kept clean. Different fish favor different conditions, so aquarists need to know the biology of every animal, and if they are working in large tanks, they might need to be able to dive.

Regular checkups

Aquarists, like this one at Sea Life Manchester in the UK, monitor their fish for signs of illness or injury. They need a special pen and board to be able to take notes under water.

Dressing for work ▲
At Sea Life Kelly Tarlton's in New Zealand, the aquarist dresses in protective gear before feeding the sharks. She checks the diving equipment and then puts on a helmet, as well as long chain mail gloves to protect her hands.

Showcasing species

Aquarists often give presentations to the public, with the help of divers in the tank. They point out the different types of fish, and explain their behavior and how they are cared for. At the Blue Planet Aquarium Aquatheatre in the UK, visitors can learn about the aquarium's Caribbean-focused exhibits, which house more than 1,500 fish.

UNDERWATER WORK

Usually, the best way aquarists can care for their animals is by taking a hands-off approach—it's important that aquatic species have minimal human contact. However, when fish are being trained or need medical care, there's no better alternative to getting in the tank with them. Aquarists make sure that the fish get used to their presence in the tanks so that their care goes as smoothly as possible.

▶ Getting up close

This aquarist at Tokyo Aquarium in Japan has plunged into a Japanese spider crab's tank so that she can check it over. These crabs can live for up to 100 years and are the world's largest crustacean (an animal with a hard shell), with a leg span of up to 12½ ft (3.8 m).

Training for touch

Interacting with humans can be stressful for animals, so aquarists help them cope with these situations. At Florida Aquarium, these aquarists are training a nurse shark to help it get used to a person's presence and touch.

FEEDING FISH AND CORAL

Earth's waters are full of a vast variety of different fish and other aquatic species, and this is often the case in aquarium tanks, too. As in the wild, competition for food is fierce, so aquarists have come up with some clever ways to make sure all the different aquatic animals in the tanks get the right type and amount of food. Some of the animals are "target fed," which means that the keepers feed them directly. Others are "scatter fed"—keepers throw larger amounts of food into the tank, and the animals feast freely on it. This aquarist at S.E.A. Aquarium in Singapore is using a long rod to target feed the fish in their California habitat.

Food prep

Each species of fish has different dietary needs. At uShaka Sea World in South Africa, an aquarist is carefully weighing out portions of food for the many aquatic animals in his care. Herbivores are fed things such as peas, lettuce, and spinach, while the carnivores feast on fish like hake, squid, and sardines.

Feeding coral

In the wild, the food that corals feed on is constantly replaced by the ebb and flow of the ocean's currents. But this does not happen in aquarium tanks. To make sure their corals get enough nutrition, aquarists use specialized equipment to target feed them, such as here at Brazil's São Paulo Aquarium.

WATERY WONDERS

Jellyfish are one of the most unusual creatures to be found in Earth's seas and oceans. Consisting of about 96 percent water, they are very delicate and have to be housed in special tanks within the aquarium. But jellyfish are also surprisingly complex, despite not having a heart, brain, or even a skeleton, and have a fascinating life cycle—in fact, it seems that some species don't ever die! When the adult form of the jellyfish (known as a medusa) decays, its cells create babies called polyps, which grow into new jellyfish. This cycle can take up to 20 years.

Spinning top

Jellyfish are kept in kreisel tanks ("kreisel" means "spinning top" in German), like this one in France's Nausicaa Aquarium. The circular flow of water stops the jellyfish from bumping into the sides of the tank.

Growing a food chain

If jellyfish don't get enough to eat, they start to shrink. To ensure a plentiful supply of food, South Africa's Two Oceans Aquarium rears shrimp to feed to their jellyfish on a daily basis.

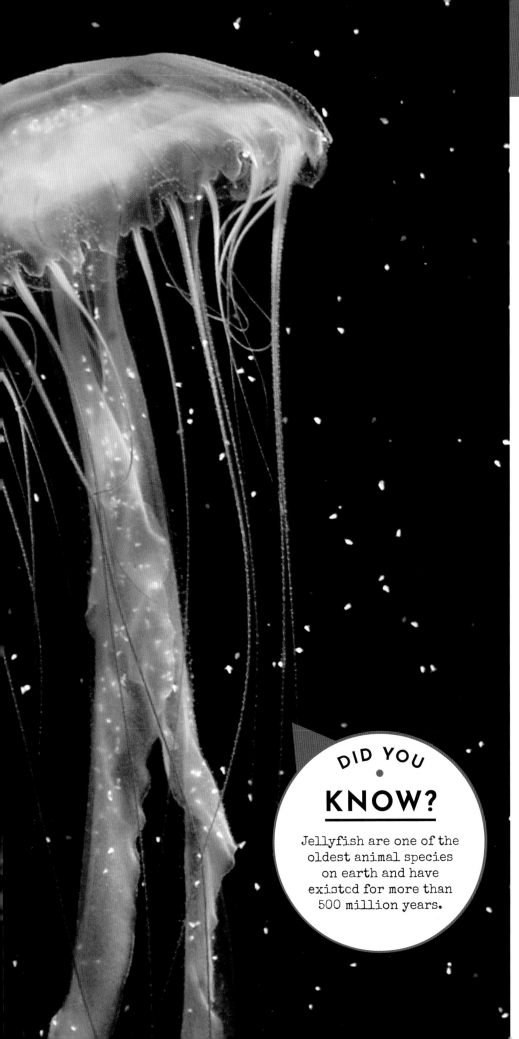

Jellyfish life cycle

It takes time and patience to grow jellyfish in an aquarium, because their life cycle can be very long. Aquarists have to fine-tune the conditions at each stage.

Polyps

1 A fertilized jellyfish egg floats through the water until it can hook onto something solid, where it grows into a polyp.

Budding polyps

2 The polyp buds to create clones of itself, forming a colony. The polyp stage can last for months or years.

◀ **Medusa**

3 The adult jellyfish is shaped like a bell, like this blackstar northern sea nettle at the Horniman Museum in the UK.

DID YOU
KNOW?

Jellyfish are one of the oldest animal species on earth and have existed for more than 500 million years.

SPECIALIST ZOOS

There is such an immense variety of wildlife on Earth that sometimes the best way to care for these animals in captivity is to specialize. Certain zoos might focus on a single animal group, such as birds or reptiles, others on animals from a particular geographical area. With such specialist knowledge, they are able to gain great insight into the animals in their care.

Korkeasaari Zoo is located on an island in Finland.

A scarlet peacock butterfly uses its distinctively patterned wings to attract a mate.

KORKEASAARI ZOO

Home to a wide range of animals from all over the world, Korkeasaari Zoo's animals do all have one thing in common. From wolverines and bactrian camels to vicunas and lynxes, they're all well suited to living in Finland's cold and sometimes harsh climate.

SINGAPORE NIGHT SAFARI

This wildlife park in Singapore opens only at night. Visitors can take a tram ride or explore the walking trails to view more than 100 different species. Conservation efforts have seen the park breed Malayan tapirs and many other threatened species.

BUTTERFLY PAVILION

Despite the name, all invertebrates are welcome at this zoo in Colorado. Butterfly Pavilion is dedicated to educating the public about the importance of invertebrates to the global ecosystem. Its range of exhibits include Chrysalis Camera, which enables people to watch butterflies emerge from their chrysalises live on webcam.

1,600

The number of tropical butterflies at the zoo

REPTILIA

Based in Ontario, Canada, Reptilia is home to more than 250 animals, such as Nile crocodiles, Burmese pythons, and Cuiver's dwarf caiman. Reptiles can often seem scary, so the zoo tries to ease its visitors' fears and help educate them about any misconceptions they may have about the animals.

AUSSIE ARK

Founded in 2011 to pull the Tasmanian devil back from the brink of extinction, Aussie Ark in New South Wales in Australia released 26 of these marsupials into a wild sanctuary in 2020. This is the first step in its plan to establish a wild population on the Australian mainland after a 3,000-year absence.

PARQUE DAS AVES

This bird park in Paraná State in Brazil is committed to the conservation of endangered birds found in the Atlantic Forest of South America. Many of these endemic species are experiencing habitat loss, and Parque das Aves is working to save and boost these wild populations.

130

The number of bird species at the park

Native to South America and parts of the Caribbean, the scarlet ibis gets its bold coloring from its diet of red crustaceans.

MORE TO SEE

▶ **INTERNATIONAL CENTRE FOR BIRDS OF PREY (ICBP)**
The ICBP near Gloucester in the UK started out as a center for falcons, dedicated to educating people about these birds. Today, it cares for all birds of prey, and its main focus is conservation, including running several successful breeding projects.

▶ **TE PUIA**
The Kiwi Conservation Centre at the Māori Arts and Crafts Institute in Rotorua, New Zealand, protects and breeds kiwis. The five species of kiwis can be found only in New Zealand. The North Island brown kiwi is the country's national emblem.

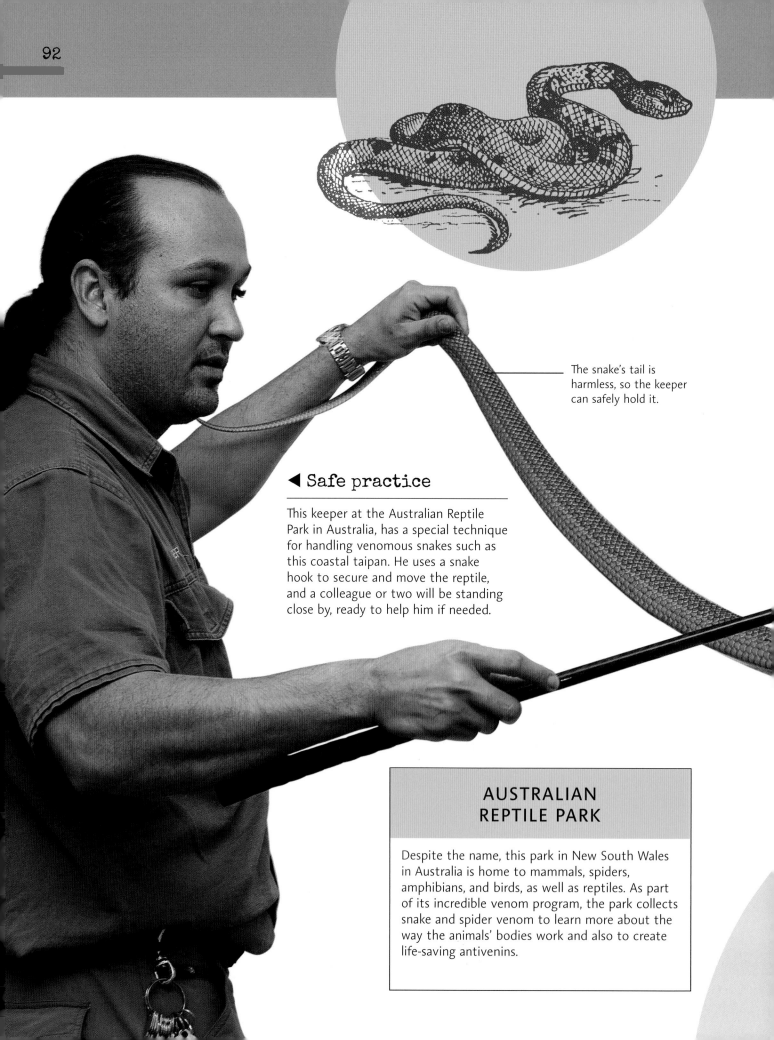

The snake's tail is
harmless, so the keeper
can safely hold it.

◀ Safe practice

This keeper at the Australian Reptile
Park in Australia, has a special technique
for handling venomous snakes such as
this coastal taipan. He uses a snake
hook to secure and move the reptile,
and a colleague or two will be standing
close by, ready to help him if needed.

AUSTRALIAN
REPTILE PARK

Despite the name, this park in New South Wales
in Australia is home to mammals, spiders,
amphibians, and birds, as well as reptiles. As part
of its incredible venom program, the park collects
snake and spider venom to learn more about the
way the animals' bodies work and also to create
life-saving antivenins.

Milking venom

To ensure good snake welfare, milking (extracting) venom is done only rarely, but the venom produced is used to make life-saving antivenins (medicines to treat people who have suffered potentially lethal bites). Antivenins also treat diseases such as cancer and diabetes.

1 An acrylic disk attached to a pole is used to carefully restrain the snake so that the keeper can gently take hold of its head.

2 The snake sinks its fangs into a latex-covered beaker. The keeper then massages its glands, causing venom to collect in the beaker.

3 The venom is transferred into small vials and sent to medical research facilities to create antivenins and other medications.

The long rod keeps the snake's fangs a safe distance away from the keeper.

DID YOU KNOW?

The coastal taipan is the longest venomous snake in Australia, reaching lengths of 5–6½ ft (1.5–2 m).

HANDLING SNAKES

Zoos are home to some of the most venomous snakes in the world. Snakes eat only small prey such as mice, but if they are mishandled or frightened, they will strike to protect themselves, giving their handler a nasty and potentially lethal bite. Keepers are trained to handle snakes in a way that maintains the welfare and safety of both the keeper and the snake.

The snake can still move around, but the hook prevents its head from reaching the keeper.

NATURAL GROOMING

Grooming helps animals keep their skin, fur, or feathers healthy by removing flakes of skin, dirt, or parasites. Animals can groom either themselves (autogrooming) or others (allogrooming). Allogrooming helps animals bond and maintain good relationships with each other.

▶ Wallowing in mud

Rolling around in mud can be fun, especially for these white rhinoceroses at Longleat safari park in the UK. But getting muddy also protects their skin from the sun's rays and biting insects. Rhinos in the wild find wallows (pools of muddy water) and use their feet and horns to enlarge the puddles. In zoos, ready-made wallows give animals a chance to interact and play together.

Dust baths

Animals often dust bathe, covering themselves in dust or sand to maintain healthy feathers, skin, or fur—just like this elephant at Chhatbir Zoo in India. Animals also do it when they are hot or want to copy what their companions do.

Scratching post

Zoos should offer animals a safe place to scratch, such as this concrete post at Germany's Hellabrunn Zoo. As well as an animal enjoying the sensation, scratching can remove parasites and dirt that has built up on the skin.

Raising cranes

The Crane School in Slimbridge in the UK has hand-reared and released more than 100 Eurasian cranes. The school minimizes human contact when teaching essential survival skills.

Model parents
Young birds require constant feeding, cleaning, and walking. This is done using a litter picker that has been made to look like an adult bird.

Lessons in foraging
Wooden models of adults show young birds how to search for food (forage). Keepers have hidden some tasty items in the enclosure for them to find.

Social skills
Once the birds start to socialize, their disguised keeper "parent" is there to stop any fights or bullying.

KEEPERS IN DISGUISE

It's usually best for animals to look after their own young, but sometimes the chicks of endangered birds are reared by hand to conserve them. Imprinting is where young animals learn what their parents look like. Zookeepers have found clever ways to disguise themselves as adult birds to prevent chicks from imprinting on them while they teach them the skills they need to deal with their environment.

▶ Northern bald ibis

At Jerez Zoo in Spain, keepers wear models of an adult northern bald ibis to hand-rear their chicks. Once common across the Middle East, northern Africa, and southern Europe, this species is now Endangered. After 30 years of conservation, its numbers have grown from 100 to 700 adults.

Ibis models mounted on cycle helmets teach hand-reared chicks to recognize adult birds, not keepers.

Glove puppets

Fewer than 100 Javan green magpies exist in the wild. Captive adults don't always make good parents, so at Prague Zoo in the Czech Republic, magpie chicks are hand-reared using glove puppets.

The northern bald ibis's genus name is *Geronticus*. It comes from the Greek for "old man," owing to the bird's unusual bald head.

FOREST PEOPLE

The name "orangutan" comes from the Malay for "person of the forest," and these hairy orange primates do indeed spend most of their lives in trees, where they feed on fruits and leaves. The three species of orangutans are Critically Endangered, and zoos have a big part to play in educating their visitors about the threat to their habitats.

▶ Tree-dwellers

Wild orangutans live high up in trees, so zoos should provide ropes and other equipment to mimic branches, allowing them to climb and swing. Adult male and female orangutans are easy to tell apart. Mature males, like this one at Dublin Zoo in Ireland, have large, disc-shaped cheek pads—apparently, the females find these very attractive!

Brainteasers

Scientists think that orangutans (and humans) are the only animals that can communicate about the past to each other, so it's really important that zoo life is stimulating for these intelligent primates. Different types of enrichment, such as the puzzle feeder this young female is playing with at Pairi Daiza Zoo in Belgium, make sure that each day presents a challenge.

Meeting the neighbors

Though they are found in the same geographical region, it's unlikely orangutans and short-clawed otters would interact in the wild—orangutans rarely come down to the ground. However, housing them together in the same zoo enclosure, such as here at Pairi Daiza Zoo in Belgium, can be stimulating and gives them an opportunity to learn about their surroundings.

PALM OIL CAMPAIGN

About 80 percent of the orangutan's habitat has been destroyed to grow palm oil, threatening the survival of the species. Zoos worldwide have campaigned to get clear labeling for sustainable palm oil (palm oil that meets our needs without affecting future generations) and ask their visitors to buy only sustainable palm oil products.

FRUIT OF THE OIL PALM TREE

COOLING OFF

When temperatures soar, even animals that are used to hot climates sometimes need help to keep cool. Outdoor enclosures have shady areas, and their inhabitants are always free to escape intense sunshine by retreating to their indoor spaces. But zoos have other inventive ways of keeping animals from overheating while they enjoy the outdoors.

BUDAPEST ZOO

Based in Hungary's capital city, Budapest Zoo and Botanical Garden is one of the oldest zoos in the world. It opened to the public in 1866, and today the zoo is a nature reserve right in the middle of a very busy city. Home to more than 1,000 animals, the zoo is arranged in seven zones, representing different geographical areas, including India, Australia, the African savanna, and Madagascar.

▶ Animal ice lollies

A giraffe at London Zoo in the UK cools off with a fruit-filled ice lolly. This treat acts as enrichment, too, as it is a way for animals to experience different textures and methods of eating their food. Because their natural habitat in Africa is hot, giraffes also have built-in ways to protect them from the sun's rays and heat.

The blue color is thought to protect the tongue from sunburn.

Fan-tastic penguins

These Humboldt penguins, native to southern Chile and Peru, are struggling in the heat, and even a dip in the pool isn't enough to stay cool. Zookeepers at London Zoo in the UK help them by placing a fan in their beach enclosure.

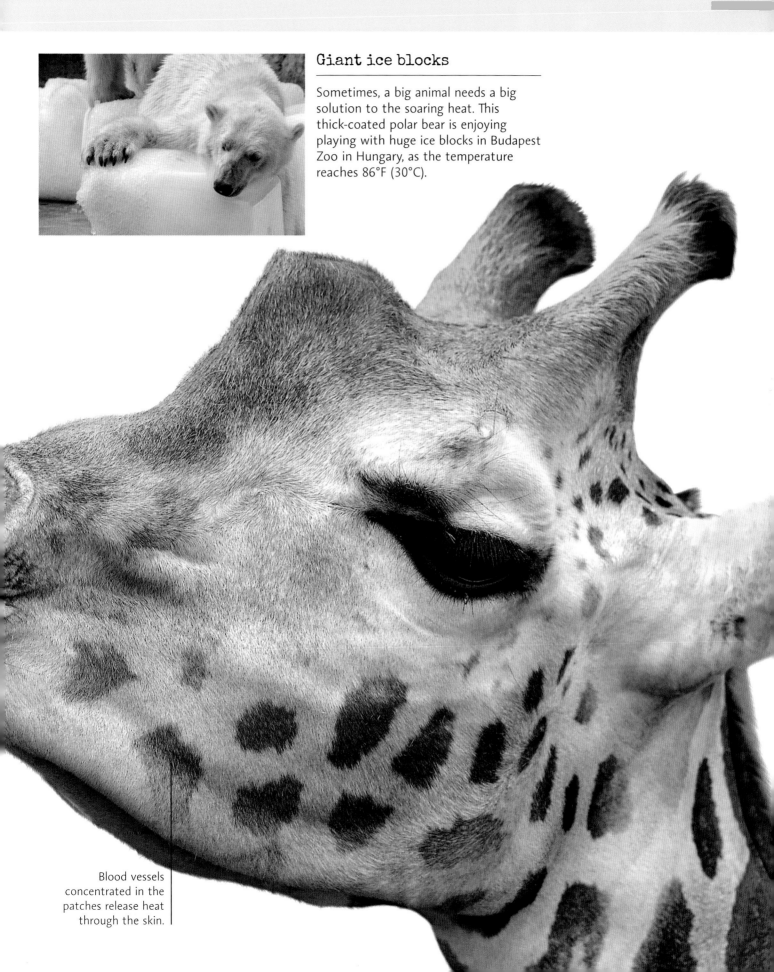

Giant ice blocks

Sometimes, a big animal needs a big solution to the soaring heat. This thick-coated polar bear is enjoying playing with huge ice blocks in Budapest Zoo in Hungary, as the temperature reaches 86°F (30°C).

Blood vessels concentrated in the patches release heat through the skin.

KEEPING WARM

While some species, such as giant pandas and polar bears, thrive in low temperatures, others are just not able to adapt to cold climates. Keepers add extra blankets or straw bedding to these creatures' indoor areas, but many of them still like to venture outside, where temperatures can be much lower than their natural habitats would be. Many zoos install underfloor heating, heated pools and rocks, and infrared lamps to keep the animals cozy and warm when temperatures start to dip.

▶ Meerkat mob

Despite their furry coats, meerkats still feel the cold. These sociable animals, which live in groups of up to 30 called "mobs," lose heat very easily because they're so small—each measures just 10–14 in (25–35 cm) and weighs less than 2 lb (1 kg). Meerkats usually love basking in the sunshine, so Magdeburg Zoo in Germany has provided the next best thing: an infrared lamp.

Flamingo hot tub

When winter comes around in Washington, DC, temperatures can drop below zero, so a dip in their very own heated pool is just what these tropical American flamingos at the Smithsonian's National Zoo need. As steam rises all around them in the chilly air, their feet are kept comfortable in the warm water.

Winter coats

Some species are better at adapting to the cold than others, and many zoos encourage this by not overheating enclosures. Although a cheetah's natural habitat is in warm African climates, it can acclimatize to the cold by growing a winter coat. With extra layers of fur, this cheetah at the Smithsonian's National Zoo can now roam outdoors even when temperatures fall.

MEXICAN LEAF FROG

In the dry, hot forests of Mexico, Mexican leaf frogs thrive even though temperatures soar. At Chester Zoo in the UK, zookeepers have been working hard to understand the breeding habits of this particular species. One-third of the world's frog species are at risk of extinction, and although the Mexican leaf frog is currently thriving, what the zookeepers have discovered will help save the species if numbers ever start to decline.

Life cycle of a Mexican leaf frog

Because ponds dry out quickly in the heat, tadpoles of the Mexican leaf frog become froglets in just five weeks—almost twice the speed of other species.

1 Mexican leaf frogs attach their eggs to plants above ponds only during the rainy season. Chester Zoo mimicked this rain to encourage the frogs to breed.

2 The transparent eggs hang together in a jelly cluster known as spawn. The embryos soon start to look like tiny tadpoles, each with a head and tail.

3 Once the tadpoles are fully developed, they hatch out of the eggs and fall into the pond below, where they start to grow rapidly into froglets.

CHESTER ZOO

Chester Zoo in the UK has around 35,000 animals, as well as botanic gardens filled with plants from all over the world. The zoo is dedicated to preventing extinction and runs conservation and research projects for all sorts of animals, including the eastern black rhino and the Philippine cockatoo.

▼ A European first

Chester Zoo managed to get two Mexican leaf frogs to breed by closely mimicking the frogs' natural Mexican habitat: very hot, with a short rainy season. Soon after came the very first tadpoles of this species ever to hatch in a European zoo, resulting in 100 healthy froglets.

These frogs have gold-speckled eyes.

Amphibians can breathe and absorb water through their skin.

DID YOU
KNOW?

Mexican leaf frogs live in temperatures of up to 104ºF (40ºC), hotter than most other frog species can handle.

KEEPING RECORDS

Zoos keep daily records that help them care for their animals. They also keep in-depth information, such as species, sex, and place of birth. This helps them identify which animals they're responsible for and to keep a track of animals that have been temporarily moved to a new zoo. These details are added to Species360, an online database, that brings together records from zoos across the world and allows keepers to access the latest information about each species.

◀ Annual stocktake

Detailed records help keepers understand animal biology. For example, regular measurements of the sea turtle at Sea Life Timmendorfer Strand in Germany teach keepers about growth rates. Collecting detailed records can be time-consuming, so some zoos choose to collect information once a year during an annual stocktake.

Daily monitoring

Keepers observe animals daily to see whether they look healthy. For animals that are hard to recognize individually, this might be all that is recorded. Zookeepers might note how animals behave in a group or react to an enrichment activity, as with this group of squirrel monkeys at London Zoo in the UK.

MEASURING ANIMALS

Weighing and measuring animals regularly helps zoos ensure that all their animals are healthy. These important figures can be compared with those from other zoos and are also used to support conservation efforts in the wild. Measurements show how an animal adapts to changes in the seasons, and they help keepers follow the growth of their animals, from when they're a tiny infant to when they're adults ready to become parents to when they're the oldest creatures in the zoo.

Penguins will stand still to be weighed if given a fish snack.

▶ Weighing in

Weight is an important way to check health and well-being. It helps zookeepers know whether an animal is getting the right amount of food—if this penguin is lighter or heavier than expected, its diet can be altered to make sure it's getting the nutrition it needs. Issues with weight can also be a sign of disease or distress, so keepers may bring in the vet for further investigations.

Different types of weighing scales are used for different kinds of animals.

DID YOU KNOW?

Penguins can't fly, but their flippers and webbed feet make them excellent, speedy swimmers.

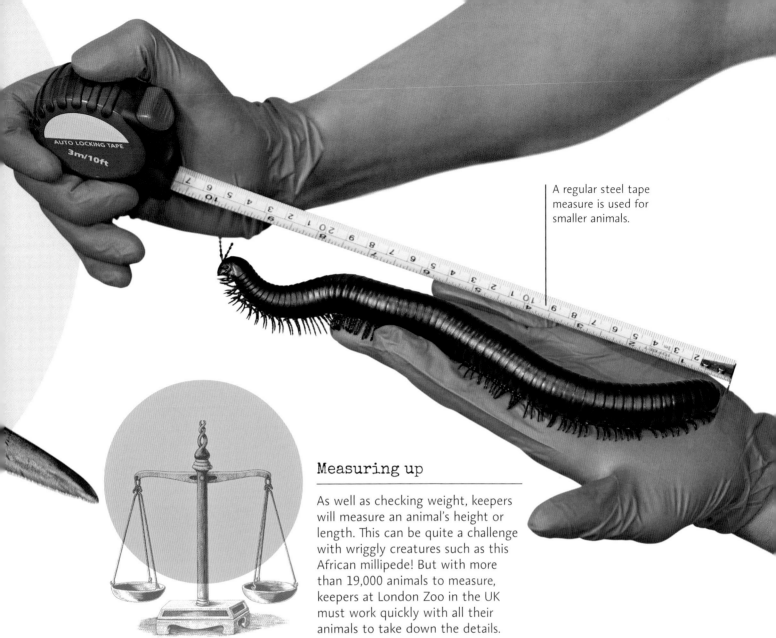

A regular steel tape measure is used for smaller animals.

AUTO LOCKING TAPE
3m/10ft

Measuring up

As well as checking weight, keepers will measure an animal's height or length. This can be quite a challenge with wriggly creatures such as this African millipede! But with more than 19,000 animals to measure, keepers at London Zoo in the UK must work quickly with all their animals to take down the details.

Tricks of the trade

Taking accurate measurements isn't always an easy task. Some animals will happily stay still, but others need a bit of encouragement. The zookeepers at London Zoo in the UK have a few tricks up their sleeves to get the measurements they need.

Reach up
This Asiatic lion is trying to get the meat its keepers have hung by a measuring board. As soon as it's fully stretched, staff can note down the animal's height.

Reach down
By placing a bucket of food on a hanging scale, keepers can quickly jot down each squirrel monkey's weight as it darts into the bucket to grab a snack.

Sit tight
Some animals don't need tricks. This African bullfrog is an easy customer, allowing a zookeeper to pop it straight onto the scales to be weighed with no fuss.

DID YOU KNOW?

Greater one-horned rhinoceroses' horns are usually 8–24 in (20–60 cm) long and can grow back if broken off.

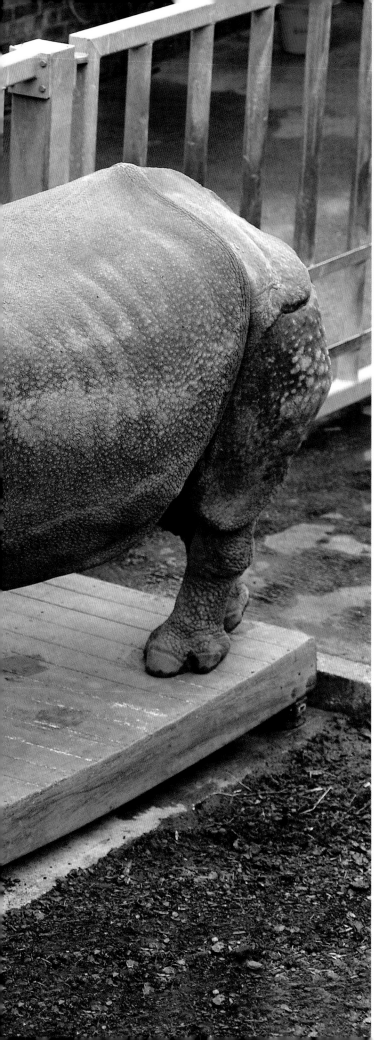

LITTLE AND LARGE

Size plays its part in the challenge to weigh animals. This female greater one-horned rhinoceros at Whipsnade Zoo in the UK needs a giant set of scales to record her weight—she tips the scales at around 3,900 lb (1,765 kg). It would be dangerous for the keepers to enter the enclosure, so they have trained the rhino to follow a target so that she can be encouraged to stand on the scales by herself—for a reward of food, of course!

Light-footed spider

Small creatures need a more sensitive set of scales to register their weight. This Mexican red-knee tarantula at London Zoo in the UK is surprisingly light—once the weight of the container has been subtracted, it will weigh in at just ½ oz (15 g).

ZOO VET

Zoo vets look after the health of animals in zoos—
they need to be expert in the biology of all the
species that live there. Vets treat and prevent
diseases, operating on animals when necessary. Their
day may involve anything from adjusting an animal's
diet plan to helping injured wildlife brought to the
zoo to recover. Zoo vets often get involved in
conservation programs in the wild, using their skills
to help sick animals in need of treatment.

Regular health checks

Vets aim to detect disease early. At
Jurong Bird Park in Singapore, listening
to a penguin's lungs regularly can help
spot signs of Aspergillosis, an infection
that is difficult to treat when advanced.

Sterile dressings
protect wounds and
keep them clean.

Darts can give a
sedative to distant
or untrained animals.

On the mend ▲
A zoo vet at the Clearwater Aquarium in
Florida in the US treats a green sea turtle
that has been hit by a boat. Boat
collisions pose a major risk to sea turtles.

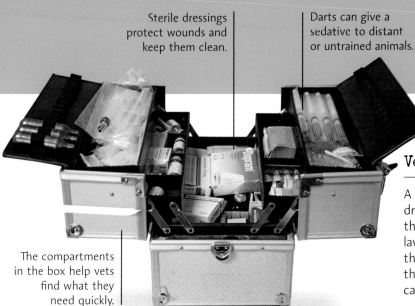

Vet kit box

A vet's kit box contains "controlled
drugs," such as the powerful medicines
that are used to sedate animals. Strict
laws mean that only vets (and those
they think are responsible) can possess
these drugs, so it's vital that the box
can be locked safely.

The compartments
in the box help vets
find what they
need quickly.

VETS IN ACTION

From telltale signs of trouble, like bleeding and limping, to subtle hints, like loss of appetite and unusual behavior, keepers are always watching out for any clues that an animal isn't feeling well. If the keepers think something isn't right, they call in the vet. Zoo vets are ready to deal with all sorts of injuries and illnesses, from bites and scratches to broken bones and serious diseases.

▶ Diagnostic lab

This baby Nile crocodile from the Crocodile Tropical Reserve in France has given the vet cause for concern, and so it's having some X-rays taken. The crocodile's mouth is painlessly wrapped with elastic bands to prevent him from nipping at the radiographer (X-ray technician).

Caring for older animals

Zoo animals generally live longer than their cousins in the wild. While this is great news, old age comes with its own problems. At Italy's Rome Zoo, a vet is thermo-scanning an elephant to check the inflammation caused by her leg arthrosis, a condition that affects the joints.

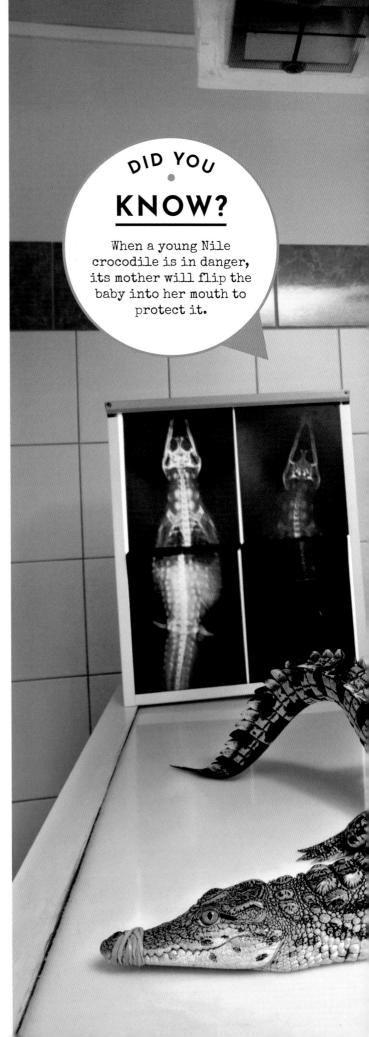

DID YOU KNOW?

When a young Nile crocodile is in danger, its mother will flip the baby into her mouth to protect it.

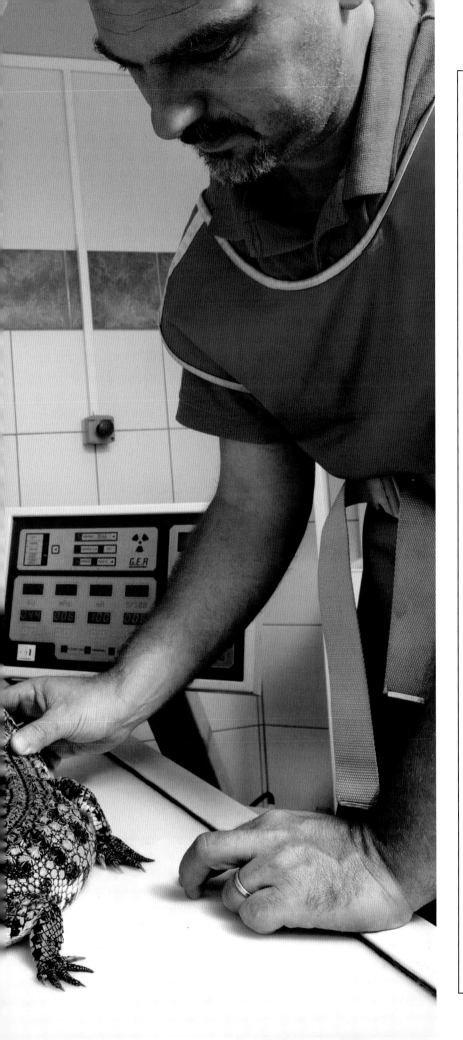

What's the problem?

At Schwerin Zoo in Germany, a female red panda has been losing weight and even some of her fur. The vet isn't sure what's wrong with her, so she's sent for a CT scan to explore the problem.

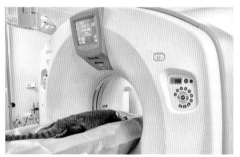

1 The zoo doesn't have a CT scanner, so she has to go to a nearby human hospital. The red panda is sedated to ensure she stays perfectly still during the scan.

2 The scan takes numerous X-rays at different angles to create a 3-D image of the red panda's bones and organs. This will help vets diagnose her condition.

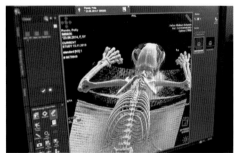

3 The scan shows that her internal organs are all in tip-top shape, but she has a growth in her nose, which will need further investigation and treatment.

GORILLA AIRLIFT

When this male western lowland gorilla started having problems with his nose, vets at Johannesburg Zoo in South Africa gave the 34-year-old gorilla antibiotics. When these didn't solve the problem, further tests were necessary. The vets decided he needed a CT scan, but the nearest scanner big enough to fit a gorilla was 40 miles (64 km) away in Pretoria, so keepers and vets had to come up with a plan to get him to the veterinary hospital quickly and safely.

1, 2, 3, 4, 5, and lift

Moving such a large animal is no mean feat. It took a team of five people to carry the 463 lb (210 kg) gorilla using a sling. They wore masks to prevent them from passing on any infections.

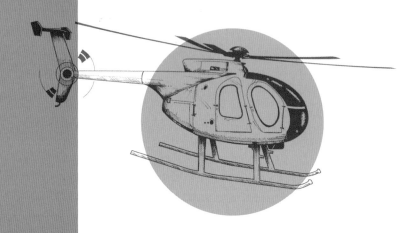

▲ Helicopter ride

Getting an early diagnosis is vital to successfully treating a sick animal. Vets thought that the trip from Johannesburg to Pretoria would have taken too long by road, so there was only one thing for it—a helicopter ride to the hospital! The vets sedated the gorilla beforehand to prevent any stress during the trip and so that he would stay perfectly still while in the CT scanner.

Up and away

With the gorilla safely looked after inside, the helicopter took off for the veterinary hospital. The CT scan showed growths inside the gorilla's nose called nasal polyps. The team performed an operation to sort out the issue.

JOHANNESBURG ZOO

Johannesburg Zoo opened in 1904, and it is now home to around 2,000 animals from more than 320 different species, such as caracals, African civets, and zebras. The "Zoo Snooze" event lets visitors take a nighttime tour and even stay the night at the zoo.

CLEANING UP

Keeping a zoo spick-and-span is not as simple as brushing things up or wiping them down. Cleaning products must be safe for use around animals, and zookeepers need to be careful not to interfere too much with the animals' habitats. Some animals, such as red pandas, mark their territory with their own scents during breeding season, and these mustn't be removed during the cleaning process.

◀ A clear view

At Frankfurt Zoo in Germany, a zookeeper uses a squeegee to clean the sea lion tank's glass, wiping away any sticky fingerprints left behind by the zoo's younger visitors so that the public can see in and the animals can see out. Aquarists (trained in the care of aquatic creatures) will also clean out the tank itself, sometimes by diving into the water.

In the enclosure

Cleaning up poo from enclosures is not the most glamorous task, but it's very important. Not only is it essential for hygiene, but analyzing an animal's poo can tell zoo staff a lot about its health, such as whether its diet is right, or if it has an infection. While mucking out this camel enclosure at Antwerp Zoo in Belgium, the keeper might do some "poo-picking"—taking samples of the camels' poo to send to a laboratory for analysis.

POO POWER

There's a lot of poo at the zoo! Every animal poos, and one elephant alone can produce up to 490 lb (220 kg) of dung every day. There's so much poo that this keeper at Rotterdam Zoo in the Netherlands is using a small dumper truck to scoop it all up. But what happens to the poo after that? Some of it goes to landfill sites and some is used as fertilizer, but Beauval Zoo in France has gone one step further, creating a poo power plant that uses this daily dung to make electricity.

POO INTO PAPER

There's no end to what poo can do! In Chiang Mai in Thailand, the POOPOOPAPER Park uses elephant poo from the local zoo and sanctuaries to make paper. This eco-friendly method not only finds a use for dung but also saves trees from being cut down for paper. The Park sells its items in the aptly named "Poo-tique."

These books are made from recycled elephant poo.

POO PAPER DRYING IN THE SUN

Making biogas

At Beauval Zoo, the animal dung is put through a process called "methanization," which creates biogas. This biogas is then used to generate electricity to heat and light parts of the zoo.

The poo is added to a liquid and placed in a mixer. Once churned, this mixture is then ready to be pumped into the factory's tank.

The tank is oxygen-free and heated to 100°F (38°C)—perfect conditions for bacteria to eat away at the mixture and produce biogas. This technician monitors the process.

The biogas turns turbines that generate electricity, which is put through a megavolt transformer. This electricity can then be used by the zoo.

Much of the work carried out by zoos happens "in the field"—in the habitats where wild animals live. Zoo staff monitor decreasing animal populations, rescue animals from floods and fires, release zoo-bred animals back into the wild, and work with local people to help save their wildlife. Animals are easier to observe in captivity than in the wild, so zoos are great places to study animal biology and behavior. The information scientists gather is shared between zoos and helps improve animal welfare and conserve threatened species.

LAB AND FIELD

WILDLIFE BIOLOGIST

Wildlife biologists study how animals live and survive. A lot of this work used to be carried out "in the field"—in the animals' natural habitat. But nowadays, some wildlife biologists spend just as much time in zoos and laboratories, researching things such as animal genetics, reproduction, and nutrition. Wildlife biologists use this research to reduce the threats to animals and to set up conservation programs to protect endangered populations both in the wild and in zoos.

Lab work

These biologists from Edinburgh Zoo in the UK are studying an antelope's poo to find out information that could be vital to safeguarding the species.

Gaining experience ▲
Becoming a wildlife biologist requires
commitment and hard work. Getting field
experience like this trainee at Gorongosa
National Park in Mozambique also helps.

In the field

Many wildlife biologists don't always see
the species they are working to save
because the animals are rare, timid, or
dangerous. Instead, they follow them
using monitoring equipment, such as
these camera traps set up by the UK's
Chester Zoo in Gashaka-Gumti National
Park in Nigeria.

Biologists set up a camera trap
(a camera triggered by movement).

There are five species of kiwis. They're related to the Australian emu and cassowary.

Native species

Zoos often help protect and conserve local wildlife that is not found elsewhere in the world. In New Zealand, Auckland Zoo has the right conditions to care for kiwis, which are unique to that country. The zoo's keepers can easily travel to the kiwi's native habitat and support efforts to protect birds living in the wild.

▼ Flagship species

Zoos want visitors to share their passion for conservation, and eye-catching animals help them do this. They become "flagship species," and protecting them also helps other animals living in the same habitat. Przewalski's horse is one example. Once Extinct in the Wild, it was reintroduced into Mongolia by the UK's Zoological Society of London.

WHAT ZOOS CAN DO

Up to a million species of plants and animals around the world are threatened with extinction. Zoos play a crucial role in supporting the conservation of animals and in educating visitors about the risks that animals and their habitats face. With so many species under threat, zoos need to choose carefully which animals to help. What space they have, the expertise of their keepers, and the local climate are some of the factors zoos think about when making their decisions. Many zoos also work to protect animals that they can't house but are still at risk of extinction.

Przewalski's horse is the only species of wild horse left in the wild.

PARTULA TREE SNAIL

Every species matters

Not all endangered animals can become flagship species, but they still need help. Partula tree snails play an important role in recycling plant debris on the islands of the Pacific. Many Partula species became extinct when humans introduced other snails that preyed on them. Edinburgh Zoo in the UK is one of many that are working together to save this species and have successfully bred and released more than 15,000 into the wild.

BIOBANKS

Many zoos, including San Diego Zoo in the US, Edinburgh Zoo in the UK, and Copenhagen Zoo in Denmark, have helped set up biobanks. Biological samples, such as sperm, eggs, and blood, are collected from endangered animals and frozen to preserve them. This genetic material might be used in the future to ensure that species don't become extinct.

FROZEN SAMPLES OF ANIMAL CELLS

HEADSTARTING IGUANAS

The blue iguana lives on the island of Grand Cayman in the Caribbean Sea. It is classified as Endangered due to habitat loss and the introduction to the island of predators such as rats, cats, and dogs. When iguana numbers dropped to below 15, zoos, governments, and wildlife organizations worked together to set up a conservation program that combined captive breeding with the "headstarting" of wild iguana hatchlings. During headstarting, hatchlings are brought into captivity until they grow large enough to survive attacks from cats and dogs—usually when they are two years old. Before release, they are microchipped, and colorful beads are threaded through their crest so that they can be easily recognized. Today, more than 400 iguanas live in three protected locations on the island.

THE IUCN RED LIST

The International Union for Conservation of Nature (IUCN) publishes The IUCN Red List of Threatened Species™ (see also p.21). A group of scientists uses a strict set of rules, such as how a species' population has changed over time, to decide whether a species is threatened or extinct. This helps inform conservation programs.

DID YOU KNOW?

The muted skin color of the Grand Cayman blue iguana brightens to a vivid blue during the mating season.

The wingspan of the Eurasian black vulture is a massive 8¾–9¾ ft (2.5–3 m).

SAVING VULTURES

Vultures perform a valuable service to the ecosystem by eating entire dead animals (including bones, feathers, and skin), which helps reduce the spread of disease. Many species of vultures, including condors and Eurasian black vultures, are endangered by human activities such as poisoning and habitat destruction. Because vultures fly over vast areas, zoos in different countries need to work together to ensure their conservation.

Bleaching feathers

To help identify released birds from a distance, conservationists harmlessly bleach some feathers. They record and share the bleach patterns with the Vulture Conservation Foundation so that birds can be recognized across different countries.

Legs are tucked up when in flight.

Condor conservation

California condors declined in the wild to about 22 birds, but San Diego Zoo in the US is one of several zoos to have helped increase their numbers to more than 500 using a process called "double clutching." An egg is removed from the nest and reared by hand. This encourages the female to lay another egg, that she rears herself.

During incubation, a light is shone through the egg (known as "candling"). This technique shows how the embryo is developing.

Newborn chicks are reared using a puppet that looks like the mother. This stops the chick from identifying people as its parents.

After release, condors continue to be monitored. This bird is having a blood sample taken to check if it has lead poisoning.

The sharp bill can tear through animal skin and flesh.

▼ Eurasian black vulture

This magnificent bird of prey once soared the skies of the whole of southern Europe—but now its numbers are fast decreasing. Planckendael Zoo in Belgium manages a European Endangered Species program for this bird. It introduces males and females to each other in "dating aviaries" and releases their young offspring into the wild.

Release

It's a hard climb to the top of the hill for these dedicated conservationists, as they prepare to release a Eurasian black vulture. The young bird is not yet able to fly, so they find it a safe place to call home until it fledges.

Feathers are dark blackish brown rather than truly black.

WELCOME BACK BILBY

The bilby is a solitary, nocturnal marsupial that lives in the deserts of Australia. An expert digger, it uses its skills to search for insects, seeds, and plant roots, at the same time creating habitats for other animals and restoring the desert ecosystem—the holes help spread air through the soil and encourage new plant growth. Once found across much of Australia, bilbies are classed as Vulnerable and are threatened by feral species such as foxes and rabbits. Recently, however, a team of conservation experts have reintroduced this unusual little creature to some of the areas where it once lived.

Loading up
A team from the Taronga Western Plains Zoo carefully loads 10 sanctuary-bred bilbies onto the plane.

Strapped in
After the bilbies have been secured in the plane, they will travel 600 miles (1,000 km) to their new desert home.

Welcoming committee
Locals, including people from the First Nations Wongkumara community, celebrate the bilbies' return after a break of 100 years.

Attaching a tag
A tracking tag is attached to each bilby's tail. This sends radio signals to an antenna, which will locate where the bilby is.

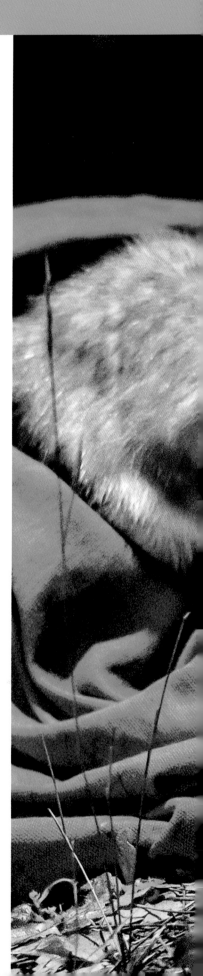

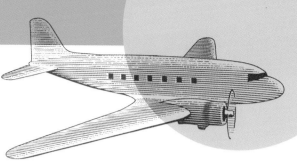

◄ Final release
The bilbies are released at night into Sturt National Park. A special fence surrounds the park, which keeps out feral animals.

Keeping tabs
Reintroduction doesn't end at release. Conservationists continue to track the bilbies through their tags, assessing how they adapt to their new environment.

TARONGA WESTERN PLAINS ZOO

This Australian zoo houses animals that need plenty of space, such as elephants, zebras, and rhinos. It plays a major role in the reintroduction of species into the wild. The zoo acknowledges the local Wiradjuri people, their country, spirit, and traditions as owners of the land where the zoo is situated.

BACK TO THE WILD

Western lowland gorillas live in the remote rain forests and swamps of central Africa. Because of poaching, habitat loss, and disease, they are now listed as Critically Endangered. Beauval Zoo in France takes part in a gorilla conservation program and has released zoo-born gorillas to the wild. This takes time, not only to prepare the animals for the long journey, but also to help them settle into their new forest homes.

1 Food for the journey
Before the gorillas set off for their new home in Gabon, their keepers pack food, including some fruit treats, for the journey.

2 Safe arrival
A keeper from Beauval Zoo reassures one of the gorillas inside its crate following their arrival at the airport in Gabon.

3 Loading the boat
The gorillas are transported across a river onto a protected island, where they can get used to life in their new environment.

4 Camera trap monitoring
The keepers observe the gorillas' progress on the island, using footage from camera traps (cameras triggered by movement).

▶ 5 Settling in
This female gorilla is now ready for release into her permanent home in the Batéké Plateau National Park.

TURTLE TRACKING

The seven species of sea turtles spend much of their lives at sea. Females come ashore every two or three years to lay eggs, but males almost never return to dry land after hatching. To learn more about turtle biology, their migrations, and the threats that endanger them, conservationists have tracked a number of individuals.

▶ Ready for release

Sea turtles live for up to 60 years. During their long lives, they face threats from plastic pollution and injuries caused by fishing nets and boats. Like many zoos and aquariums, uShaka Sea World in South Africa takes in injured animals (such as this loggerhead turtle) and helps them recover before releasing them again. This one will have a satellite tag so that its progress can be tracked.

USHAKA SEA WORLD

Made up of 32 tanks, uShaka Sea World in South Africa is the fifth-largest aquarium in the world. Based around five shipwrecks, its spectacular array of fish includes ragged-toothed and hammerhead sharks as well as local honeycomb morays, dolphins, and seals. Visitors can snorkel or dive into the protected ocean lagoon for an up-close experience.

DID YOU KNOW?

A turtle hatchling's sex depends on nest temperature. Warm nests produce females; cool ones produce males.

Attaching a tracker

Satellite trackers do no harm, but they need to be attached firmly, as with this olive ridley turtle, so that they don't become dislodged after release.

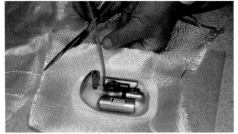

A satellite tag, including glue and waterproof sealant, weighs less than 2 percent of an adult female's body weight, which is about 80 lb (35 kg).

The turtle's carapace (upper shell) is cleaned and lightly sanded to ensure the glue will fix the tag in place permanently. Waterproof sealant is then applied.

With the tracker in place, the turtle is ready for release into a safe spot. She makes her own way into the sea and may return here later to lay her eggs.

Habitat loss

Bushfires are a natural part of Australian ecosystems. Fire regenerates some native plants, and Australia's First Peoples have traditionally used bushfires to manage the land. But recent fires have been so severe that they've destroyed the trees that provide koalas with food and shelter.

On the front line

A wildlife rescuer holds an injured koala he has saved from a burning forest, before passing it over to zoo staff for treatment. Together with firefighters and volunteers, animal rescuers provide essential support to injured animals, helping them receive care as quickly as possible.

This koala has received burns to its face.

Its burnt paws will need to be treated and bandaged.

KOALA RESCUE

Climate change is leading to more frequent extreme weather events, such as heatwaves, drought, and flooding. In Australia, hotter and drier conditions increase the risk of bushfires. Conservationists and volunteers play an important role in rescuing and treating the animals, including many koalas that are caught up in these devastating fires.

▶ Safe haven

Vets working for Zoos Victoria in south-eastern Australia visited areas devastated by bushfires. The recovery team provided care for injured animals, relocating those that needed intensive treatment to Healesville Sanctuary.

Injury care

In 2020, as many as 5,000 koalas were killed in the bushfires. Survivors suffered from burns, as with this koala, and smoke inhalation. Treatment can be long-lasting—a koala treated at Taronga Zoo in Sydney needed complicated surgery and more than nine months of rehabilitation.

Thick gray-brown fur gives koalas a bear-like appearance.

Eucalyptus leaves are so low in nutritional value that koalas have to spend many hours a day eating.

WILDLIFE PARKS

Not quite a zoo, not quite a nature reserve, a wildlife park is usually set across large expanses of land, which allows the animals freedom to roam in conditions that closely resemble their native habitats. Some wildlife parks have animals from all around the world, while others focus their efforts on protecting threatened species close to home.

Secretary birds hunt on foot. In a day, they can walk up to 20 miles (32 km) to find food.

SAN DIEGO ZOO SAFARI PARK

Set across 12 different habitat zones, this safari park has more than 300 different animal species. The "Flightline Safari" lets you soar across its savanna habitat on a zip wire 130 ft (40 m) above the ground.

Longleat House is an old manor house dating back to the 1500s.

These deer are shedding some of their hair to prepare for warmer weather on the way.

LONGLEAT

Visitors can drive themselves through this safari park in Wiltshire in the UK and wind their way past tigers, lions, and cheetahs to get a glimpse of huge white rhinos and zebras—but they have to be careful that monkeys don't take off with their windshield wipers!

THE WILDS

Set above an old coal mine, this wildlife park in Ohio educates its visitors about nature and encourages everyone to care for the environment through educational activities and its volunteering programs.

9,880
The number of acres used by the park

FEATHERDALE WILDLIFE PARK

This wildlife park in Sydney is entirely dedicated to animals native to Australia. From koalas and kangaroos to wombats and dingoes, more than 2,000 Australian animals roam around the park's three open enclosures.

260

The number of different species at the park

ZOOLOGICAL CENTER RAMAT GAN

Located in Tel Aviv in Israel, the safari park's animals roam across the park in an environment that reflects their native habitat. With more than 200 species, you can see many animals native to Africa and Asia, such as mandrills, fennec foxes, and Nile crocodiles.

CHIMELONG SAFARI PARK

More than 20,000 animals live at this huge safari park near Guangzhou in China, including lots of rare species like this herd of golden takins. A conservation center, Chimelong Safari Park works to instill visitors with a love of nature. This wildlife park even hit the headlines in 2014 when a very rare event took place: panda triplets were born!

MORE TO SEE

▶ NORTHWEST TREK WILDLIFE PARK

This wildlife park in Washington State is dedicated to animals from the northwest of the country. You can travel through the park to see moose, bison, and caribou, or step into Eagle Passage to view bald eagles in their natural habitat.

▶ RIVER SAFARI

It's mostly marine life at this wildlife park in Singapore, with aquatic habitats to match. Exhibits like Ganges River, Mekong River, and Amazon Flooded Forest mirror their real-world counterparts to house animals native to those environments.

PREVENTING POACHING

Many animals and plants are taken from the wild and sold—sometimes illegally, when it's known as poaching. Legal and illegal wildlife trade causes problems when it's not sustainable, meaning that the number of animals left in the wild starts to decline. Poaching is one of the biggest threats to species survival. To protect threatened species, some governments regulate or ban international wildlife trade using an agreement called the Convention on International Trade in Endangered Species (CITES). Zoos around the world work with CITES to stop poaching and the illegal wildlife trade.

The trunk is used to breathe, smell, touch, lift objects, and make noise.

▶ Precious ivory

Elephant tusks are made of ivory. This hard, white material is often carved into ornaments, jewelry, and piano keys. African and male Asian elephants have the largest ivory tusks and so are targeted by poachers.

Sending a message

Since 1979, elephant populations have declined by more than 50 percent, largely due to the ivory trade. Some countries have chosen to destroy illegally seized ivory to highlight the devastating impact its trade has had on elephant populations.

Most of an elephant's skin is very tough and is 1 in (2.5 cm) thick.

Elephants use their tusks for feeding and digging.

Tracing illegal trade

Asian elephant ivory trade was banned in 1975, but ivory is still traded in Asia. So where does the ivory come from? Edinburgh Zoo's WildGenes laboratory in the UK works with governments, conservation organizations, and other zoos to analyze the genetic identity of ivory recovered from illegal trading. This helps pinpoint where in the world the tusks were taken from so that the poachers can be found.

Drilling ivory
Scientists drill into the tusk to get DNA samples. All living things have their own unique DNA, which holds information about that individual.

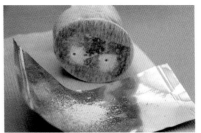

Gathering evidence
By comparing DNA samples from tusks recovered from different shipments, scientists can find out where the ivory has come from.

PROTECTING
PANGOLINS

The eight species of pangolins are thought to be the most poached mammals on Earth. They are sold and transported around the world because some people mistakenly believe their scales have health benefits. A startled pangolin, like this Temminck's ground pangolin, will roll up into a ball, exposing only its sharp scales to potential predators. Although it's an effective defense against other animals, this behavior doesn't protect the pangolin from human poachers. Luckily, this pangolin was rescued from poachers by park rangers at Gorongosa National Park in Mozambique, who later released it back into the wild. Boise Zoo has a long-term conservation partnership with the park, helping support the animals that live there.

Saving the Sunda pangolin

The Sunda pangolin is found throughout southeast Asia and is Critically Endangered due to poaching. Nashville Zoo and Newquay Zoo in the UK support the conservation charity Save Vietnam's Wildlife to protect, rescue, rehabilitate, and release Sunda pangolins.

WORKING WITH PEOPLE

Conservation programs work really well when they support both the animals under threat and the people who live alongside them. Zoos work closely with communities across the world to identify the dangers that species face and to develop the best ways to conserve them.

▶ Saving macaques

Selamatkan Yaki, which means "Save Macaques" in the Indonesian language, is the name of a program that is trying to save the Critically Endangered Sulawesi crested black macaque, found only in northern Sulawesi in Indonesia. The program is supported by zoos such as Paignton Zoo in the UK and Rotterdam Zoo in the Netherlands, and local children play an important role, both learning and teaching others about the threats of overhunting and habitat loss.

Making it fun

The program trains young ambassadors at Yaki Youth Camps, fun-filled events that focus on the positive results of conservation. Yaki ambassadors go on to spread the message to their school, community, and friends and family.

Fun activities help spread the conservation message.

This girl has made a macaque mask.

ROTTERDAM ZOO

One of the oldest zoos in the Netherlands, Rotterdam Zoo had to find a new site after bombing in World War II damaged the original zoo. It houses more than 180 species and is a leading zoo for the conservation and breeding of threatened animals such as the Lesser Antillean iguana.

DID YOU

KNOW?

Sulawesi is home to many species found only on the island, including a curious little cow called an anoa.

SULAWESI
CRESTED BLACK
MACAQUE

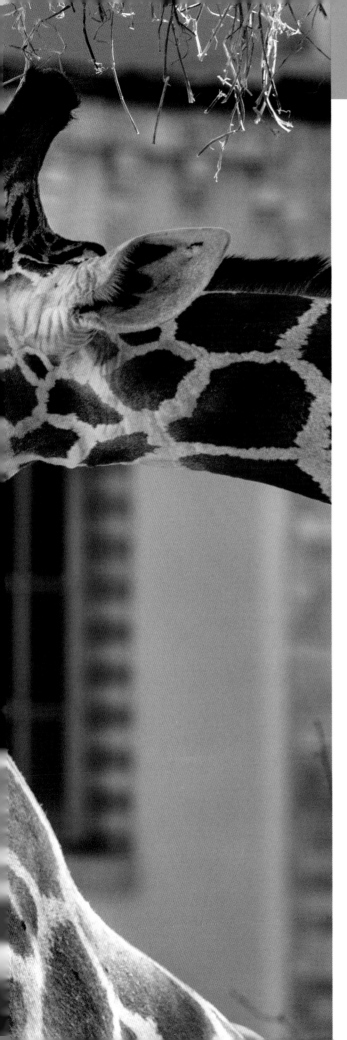

STUDYING ANIMALS

Conducting research is a key goal for most zoos, and what better place to start than by learning from the animals in their collections? Observing animal behavior can teach scientists and conservationists a great deal. Zoos use the information to adjust how they look after their animals. What they find out can also improve the conservation of animals in their natural habitats.

◀ Close observations

When researchers in Africa were unable to analyze their data about giraffe behavior, they sent a GPS headset to Berlin Zoo in Germany. One of its animals wore this while going about its daily routine, which provided details about when giraffes eat, sleep, and are most active. The researchers were able to use this information to help protect giraffes in the wild.

A puzzling problem

At Berlin Zoo in Germany, a camera placed inside a puzzle box records how this chimp uses a stick as a tool to get to the food inside. It's important that observations are done discreetly, as the presence of humans may affect how an animal behaves.

GIANT PANDA WATCH

Staff at the Smithsonian's National Zoo watch over their giant pandas from a high-tech observation center filled with TV monitors, which helps them understand these fascinating animals without disturbing their natural behavior. This giant panda is about to make the journey to China, so staff are making especially sure it's in tip-top condition for its flight.

DID YOU KNOW?

The giant panda's species name, *Ailuropoda melanoleuca*, means "black-and-white cat foot."

Return to China

It's time for another giant panda to fly home to China. All giant pandas are owned by the Chinese government and are individually loaned out to zoos around the world. This one has been housed at the Smithsonian's National Zoo, but it's now being flown to a special reserve in Chengdu. Here, it will become part of China's breeding and conservation program—although giant pandas are still classed as Vulnerable, happily their numbers in the wild are increasing.

AMPHIBIANS IN CRISIS

Almost half of the 8,000 known species of amphibians are threatened with extinction. One of the main causes for this is a highly contagious disease caused by the chytrid (pronounced "kit-trid") fungus, which affects the animals' skin and leads to their death. Zoos around the world are working together to save amphibians, recovering endangered species from the wild and moving them to safety in captivity. Conservationists have set up captive breeding programs and are trying to learn about the disease in an attempt to find a cure.

GAIAZOO

Calling itself the most beautiful zoo in the Netherlands, GaiaZOO is home to more than 150 different species. The exhibits are organized in geographical areas such as the Rainforest and African Savannah, and the zoo educates its visitors about the importance of rare local wildlife, such as the European hamster.

▶ Fire salamander

Once common across central Europe, fire salamanders are now hard to find—despite their bright coloring. In recent years, the chytrid fungal infection has caused the salamander population in the Netherlands to drop by about 95 percent. To safeguard the remaining animals, GaiaZOO in the Netherlands has removed salamanders from the wild and has kept them in a safe environment that is free from the fungus.

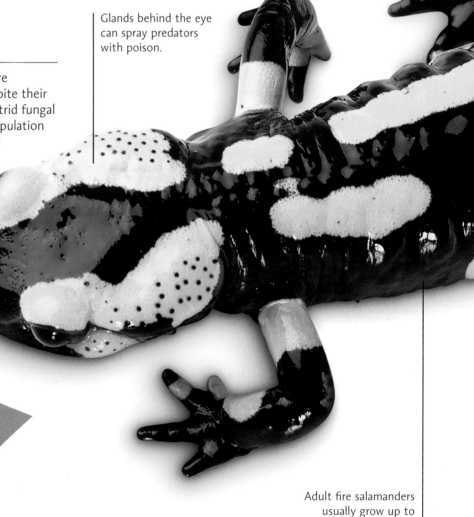

Glands behind the eye can spray predators with poison.

Adult fire salamanders usually grow up to 12 in (30 cm) in length.

DID YOU KNOW?

Some fire salamander species retain their eggs inside them so appear to give birth to live young.

Breathable skin
Many amphibians, including fire salamanders, have thin, moist skin that allows gases and liquids to pass through it easily. This helps them breathe and take in water but also makes them very sensitive to pollution or diseases in their environment. The chytrid fungus affects their skin, preventing it from working properly.

If the tail, a toe, or a leg breaks, the salamander can grow a new one.

Glands in the skin can produce harmful toxins if the salamander is touched.

Taking a swab

Chytrid fungus is very contagious, spreading through touch or water. Some amphibians can carry the fungus without becoming sick. To ensure the animals are looked after in an infection-free environment, zoos swab and test each individual to be certain that they don't infect the rest of the group.

Under the microscope

There are two types of chytrid fungus, and together these have caused the decline of more than 500 amphibian species. One type of fungus seems to thrive in cool European climates, and the other flourishes in hot and wet tropical environments. Scientists are studying the different fungus strains and their effects on salamander skin to find out how to combat them.

POO SLEUTHING

Why would a zoo have a freezer full of poo? Because there is a lot you can discover, such as whether an animal has a disease, is pregnant, or is stressed. Poo contains hormones—chemicals that scientists can analyze to find out about an animal's health. The Smithsonian's National Zoo has a special lab for analyzing hormones. It receives samples of poo from many different animals, which it stores in freezers until they are ready to be processed.

DID YOU KNOW?

Rabbits eat their soft droppings. These contain important nutrients, which are an essential part of their diet.

▶ Why poo?

Hormones travel around the body in blood but can also be found in saliva, hair, and pee and poo. The easiest and least invasive way to check an animal's hormones is by collecting, processing, and analyzing its poo. This is especially important, as hormones may need to be tested regularly. From piles of elephant dung to little mounds of deer droppings, there's always plenty of poo in a zoo!

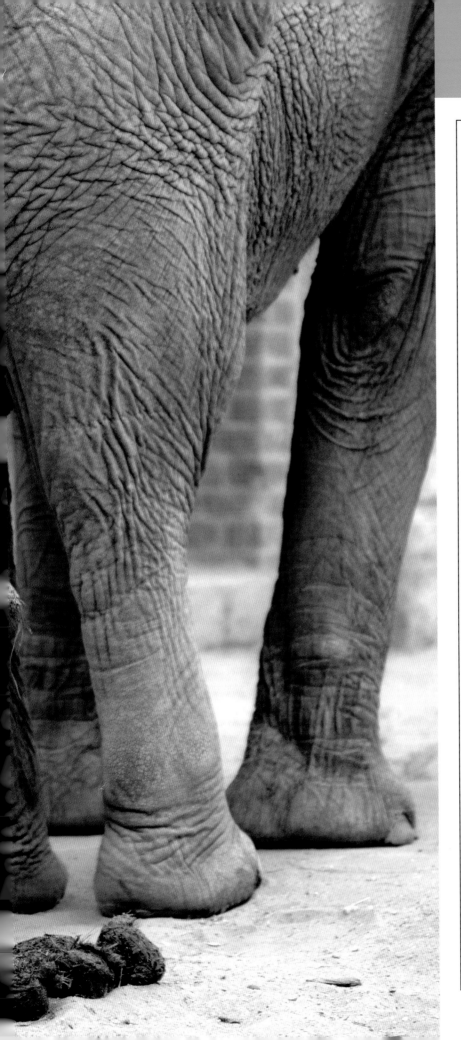

Preparing a poo sample

The scientists in the lab don't analyze hormones by looking directly at the poo itself. Instead, they need to isolate the hormones from the poo before they can run the tests.

The poo comes in little bags, placed in boxes labeled with the animal's name and the date of collection. Samples are stored in a freezer until needed.

The samples are first freeze-dried to remove all the moisture. Then the bags are bashed with a mallet to break the poo down into a fine dust.

This poo dust is tipped into a test tube containing an alcohol solution. The tube is then spun on a vortex machine to release the hormones into the liquid.

GLOSSARY

Words in **bold** appear elsewhere in the Glossary.

Aquarist
Someone who studies and cares for **aquatic** life

Aquatic
An animal or plant that grows or lives in water

Bacteria
Tiny organisms that can sometimes cause disease

Behavior
The way an animal acts, such as what and how it eats, whether it hunts, likes to live in groups, and so on

Biology
The science of living things, including how life is created and maintained; a person studying biology is called a biologist

Breeding
The process of producing baby animals

Camouflage
Colors, patterns, or shapes that allow an animal to blend in with its surroundings

Captivity
Refers to animals kept in human care, such as in zoos

Carnivore
An animal that eats meat

Climate
General weather conditions; climate change refers to the rise in Earth's temperature, leading to more extreme weather, e.g., droughts, flooding

Clone
An animal that has been created from the cells of another animal and is identical to it

Clutch
The number of eggs laid by a bird, reptile, or amphibian at one time

Conservation
Saving and protecting animals and the environment

Contraception
Medicine to prevent pregnancy

Crustacean
An animal with a hard shell and several pairs of legs, usually living in water, e.g., a crab

CT scan
An abbreviation of Computer Tomography, used for diagnosing problems inside the body

DNA
The substance that gives each living thing its characteristics

Ecosystem
Animals and plants living in the same **habitat**, and the relationship between them

Embryo
An unborn animal at the first stage of its development

Enclosure
The place in a zoo where animals are kept; see also **Exhibit**

Endemic
Species that are **native** to an area and aren't found anywhere else in the world

Enrichment
Activities or objects that allow animals to use their skills

Exhibit
An area of the zoo where animals can be seen by the public; see also **Enclosure**

Extinction
When there are no living members of an animal **species** left

Feral
Refers to domestic animals, such as cats and dogs, that are not cared for by people but are living wild

Fertile
Able to have babies

Fertilization/ Fertilize
The joining of an egg and a **sperm** to create an **embryo**

Fledge
Grow the feathers needed for flying

Genetic
Concerned with the genes that control physical characteristics, growth, and development; genes are made up of **DNA**

Genus
A group of **species** that have similar features, with names given in Latin, e.g., tigers, leopards, and lions are part of the *Panthera* genus

Gland
An **organ** in the body that produces chemical substances

Grooming
Removing flakes of skin, dirt, or parasites from skin, fur, or feathers to keep clean.

Habitat
The place or environment where an animal naturally lives

Hatch
To emerge from an egg or pupa; a hatchling is a recently hatched baby animal

Herbivore
An animal that eats plant material, including trees, fruits, and vegetables

Horticulture
Studying and growing plants

Inbreeding
The repeated **breeding** of animals that are closely related

Incubation
Keeping an egg warm until the baby **hatches**

Insectivore
An animal that eats insects

Larva/larvae
The stage before an insect changes into its adult form

Litter
A group of babies born to an animal at the same time

Marine
Describes animals and plants that live in the sea

Microchip
An electronic device placed under the skin that is used to identify an animal

Migration
Moving from one place to another at a particular time or season

Native
Animals and plants that live or grow in a place naturally and weren't brought there by people

Nocturnal
Animals that are active mainly at night

Nutrients
Substances that enable animals and plants to survive, grow, and reproduce, e.g., vitamins and protein

Nutrition
The process of taking food into the body and absorbing **nutrients**

Organ
A part of the body, such as the lungs or heart, that carries out a specific job, such as breathing or pumping blood

Pack
A group of dogs or wolves that hunt together

Parasite
An animal that lives off another animal (either inside or on the body), often doing harm

Photosynthesis
The method that plants use to make their food

Poaching
The illegal capture and trade of animals

Pollution
Dirty or harmful substances in the environment

Predator
An animal that hunts and kills other animals (known as **prey**)

Prey
An animal that is hunted and killed by another animal (known as a **predator**)

Pride
A group of lions

Primate
A mammal such as a monkey or an ape that has hands or feet that can hold things, and a large brain

Rehabilitation
Helping an animal to become healthy again

Reproduction
Producing baby animals; if assistance from humans is needed, it is called artificial reproduction

Safety population
A group of animals (**species**) managed in zoos to protect them from extinction

Sedate
To give medication to make an animal sleepy

Species
Animals within a **genus** that have very similar characteristics; names are given in Latin, with the genus name first, e.g., the species name for tiger is *Panthera tigris*

Sperm
Tiny cell produced by male animals that can enter the female's egg to **fertilize** it

Subspecies
A group of animals within a **species** that have been separated and so change (sometimes only slightly), e.g., the Amur tiger and the Sunda tiger are two subspecies of tiger

Thermo-scan
A way of measuring heat inside the body

Ultrasound scan
Image created by sound waves that is used for diagnosing medical conditions and for monitoring unborn babies

Unfertilized
Eggs that have not been in contact with **sperm**

Uterus
In mammals, the part of the female body where babies develop

Venom
A poisonous liquid produced by animals such as snakes to protect themselves or to kill prey

Welfare
A measure of how an animal feels and whether its environment can satisfy its needs

X-ray
Used to examine bones or **organs** inside the body

INDEX

ACKNOWLEDGMENTS

DK would like to thank the many zoos and aquariums who gave advice and offered their photographs free of charge during a time of great difficulty.

Also thanks to the following for their contributions:
Frankie Lawrence-Thompson (BIAZA), Lauren Florisson (EAZA), and Martin Zordan (WAZA) for reaching out to zoos around the world; Katharina Herrmann for her assistance with photographs and stories; Sheila Roe and Louise Grossfeldt for their advice; Kim Evans and SEA LIFE Kelly Tarlton's Aquarium for permission to reproduce their photographs; the IUCN for their assistance; Richard Gibson for his advice on snakes; Michelle Staples and Joe Lawrence for additional design; Tom Booth for additional editing; Caroline Stamps for proofreading; Carron Brown for indexing; Steve Crozier, Pankaj Sharma, Jagtar Singh, and Neeraj Bhatia for retouching; Rituraj Singh for additional picture research; Suhita Dharamjit and Priyanka Sharma-Saddi for the jacket.

The publisher would like to thank the following for their kind permission to reproduce their photographs:
(Key: a-above; b-below/bottom; c-center; f-far; l-left; r-right; t-top)
1 Shutterstock.com: Andrey Oleynik (c).
2 Alamy Stock Photo: Antiqueimages (cr); Darling Archive (clb). **naturepl.com:** Roland Seitre (ca). **Shutterstock.com:** Evgeny Turaev (cb). **3 123RF.com:** fotointeractiva (cl). **Alamy Stock Photo:** Antiqueimages (cb). **Dreamstime.com:** Andrii Oliinyk (crb).
4 123RF.com: andreyoleynik (cr). **Dreamstime.com:** Andrii Oliinyk (tr). **Getty Images/iStock:** Andrii-Oliinyk (bc). **5 123RF.com:** andreyoleynik (tr). **Getty Images/iStock:** Andrii-Oliinyk (br). **Shutterstock.com:** Evgeny Turaev (tc). **6 Dreamstime.com:** Andrii Oliinyk (cra). **Shutterstock.com:** Morphart Creation (tc). **7 123RF.com:** andreyoleynik (bl). **Getty Images/iStock:** Andrii-Oliinyk (cra). **Shutterstock.com:** Andrey Oleynik (cr). **9 Shutterstock.com:** Evgeny Turaev (cb, cb). **10–11 Wildlife Reserves Singapore:** (b). **11 Alamy Stock Photo:** Hemis (tl). **12 Alamy Stock Photo:** Ian Gunning (br); Rosanne Tackaberry (cr). **Getty Images/iStock:** Andrii Oliinyk (tr).
13 123RF.com: fullempty (tr). **Shutterstock.com:** becauz gao (tc). **Wikipedia:** Javier Yaya Tur (cr). **14–15 Alamy Stock Photo:** Heritage Image Partnership Ltd. **15 Dublin Zoo:** courtesy of The National Library of Ireland (bc). **Getty Images:** Werner Forman/Universal Images Group (tc). **16–17 Alamy Stock Photo:** Marius Becker/dpa picture alliance archive. **18 Alamy Stock Photo:** Reading Room 2020 (tr). **Getty Images:** ROSLAN RAHMAN/AFP (cr). **naturepl.com:** Andrew Peacock (br). **19 naturepl.com:** Eric Baccega (cr). **Tierpark Hellabrunn:** Marc Müller (tr). **20 Alamy Stock Photo:** Dave Watts (clb). **naturepl.com:** D. Parer & E. Parer-Cook (bl). **20–21 Dreamstime.com:** Isselee (c). **21 123RF.com:** mohd hairul fiza musa (tr). **22 Dorling Kindersley:** Thomas Marent (br). **naturepl.com:** Melvin Grey (c).
23 123RF.com: Brian Kinney/ivantagan (tl). **Dublin Zoo:** Patrick Bolger (br). **25 123RF.com:** andreyoleynik (cb). **26–27 Smithsonian's National Zoo:** (all).
28 Chester Zoo: (c, bc). **Dan Pearlman:** (cb). **28–29 Dan Pearlman:** (c). **29 Chester Zoo:** (ca). **Dan Pearlman:** (tc, cr, bc). **30 Alamy Stock Photo:** dpa picture alliance (clb).
Philadelphia Zoo: (crb). **30–31 Alamy Stock Photo:** Hemis (t). **31 Alamy Stock Photo:** Jane Rix (clb). **Dreamstime.com:** Michael Williams (crb). **32 Alamy Stock Photo:** agefotostock/Antonio D´Albore (c). **Shutterstock.com:** Oscity (clb). **32–33 Alamy Stock Photo:** agefotostock/Antonio D´Albore (c). **33 Alamy Stock Photo:** EThamPhoto (tr). **Dreamstime.com:** Mario Krpan (cr). **Shutterstock.com:** EPA/Patrick B Kraemer (crb). **34 Alamy Stock Photo:** Xinhua (cl); ZUMA Press, Inc. (tr). **Columbus Zoo and Aquarium:** Grahm S. Jones (crb).
Maxime Thué: (clb). **35 Royal Burgers' Zoo:** Jan Vermeer (tl). **Salzburg Zoo:** (clb). **Taipei Zoo:** (cra, cr). **Wikipedia:** Pierre Dalous (cb).
36–37 Getty Images: AFP/Patrick Kovarik (r).
36 Smithsonian's National Zoo: (clb).
38 São Paulo Aquarium: (clb). **38–39 Dreamstime.com:** Elenaphotos. **39 uShaka Sea World:** (cra, crb). **40 Alamy Stock Photo:** Jason Knott (crb); Stephanie Starr (clb); Jan Wlodarczyk (cra); Markus Thomenius (br).
41 Alamy Stock Photo: FB-StockPhoto-1 (tr).
Aquamarine Fukushima: (tl).
Atlanterhavsparken: Finn Refsnes (clb); H. Valderhaug (bl). **42 naturepl.com:** Piotr Naskrecki (cra). **42–43 Alamy Stock Photo:** agefotostock/Marcin Lyszkiewicz (b).
43 Alamy Stock Photo: 19th era (tc).
naturepl.com: Edwin Giesbers (cla).
Shutterstock.com: bluedog studio (cr).
44–45 Getty Images: Matt Cardy (c).
44 Zoos Victoria: (bc); Rohan Cleave (bl, br).
45 Alamy Stock Photo: Darling Archive (tc).
Shutterstock.com: Gummy Bear (bc). **Zoos Victoria:** Rohan Cleave (bl). **46 Wildlife Reserves Singapore:** (clb, bl). **46–47 Getty Images:** The Sydney Morning Herald.
47 naturepl.com: Eric Baccega (cra).
Shutterstock.com: yuRomanovich (br).
49 Dreamstime.com: Andrii Oliinyk (cb).
50–51 Getty Images: Hugh R Hastings (t).
50 Getty Images: ROSLAN RAHMAN/AFP (br). **51 Columbus Zoo and Aquarium:** Grahm S. Jones (bl). **52 Alamy Stock Photo:** Eric Gevaert (c). **Columbus Zoo and Aquarium:** Grahm S. Jones (cra).
53 BluePlanetArchive.com: Suzan Meldonian (br); Gerald Nowak (cra). **RZSS:** (cl, cb). **54 Alamy Stock Photo:** Antiqueimages (cra). **Getty Images:** AFP/Henning Bagger. **55 Alamy Stock Photo:** Auscape International Pty Ltd/Jean-Paul Ferrero (clb). **Dreamstime.com:** Anankkml (cla). **56 naturepl.com:** Eric Baccega (cl).
56–57 naturepl.com: Eric Baccega.
58–59 Smithsonian's National Zoo: (l).
59 Shutterstock.com: Evgeny Turaev (br).
Smithsonian's National Zoo: (c, cb).
60 Dreamstime.com: Iryna Zaichenko (tr).
60–61 Alamy Stock Photo: UPI/Pat Benic (bl). **61 Smithsonian's National Zoo:** (all).
62–63 Getty Images: Joern Pollex.
62 Paignton Zoo: Eleanor Stobbart (clb).
64 Dreamstime.com: Frantic00 (cla).
Smithsonian's National Zoo: (clb).
64–65 Alamy Stock Photo: PA Images/Lewis Whyld (b). **65 Shutterstock.com:** nata_danilenko (cr). **66 Shutterstock.com:** John_Silver (clb). **66–67 Paignton Zoo:** Cathy Oetegenn. **68–69 Getty Images:** Mark Kolbe.
68 ZSL London Zoo: Harriet Whittaker (clb).
70 Alamy Stock Photo: agefotostock (tc); Paul Kingsley (clb); Commission Air (br).
Getty Images: Ian Waldie (cl). **Pretoria Zoo:** (tr). **71 Alamy Stock Photo:** EQRoy (tr); Kieran McManus (clb). **Getty Images:** Blom UK (cla). **Shutterstock.com:** marcobrivio.photo (ca). **Smithsonian's National Zoo:** Jim Jenkins (ftr). **72 Alamy Stock Photo:** Peter Ekvall (bl). **72–73 Precision Behavior:** A. Millwood-Lacinak (c). **73 Paignton Zoo:** Miriam Haas (crb). **Wildlife Reserves Singapore:** (tr). **74–75 Smithsonian's National Zoo. 74 Alison Allen Photography/Blackpool Zoo:** (cl). **76 123RF.com:** andreyoleynik (cb). **Longleat Safari Park:** Ian Turner (clb). **76–77 Alamy Stock Photo:** Sueddeutsche Zeitung Photo. **77 Alamy Stock Photo:** Sueddeutsche Zeitung Photo (crb). **Zoo Zagreb:** (cra). **78 Alamy Stock Photo:** dpa picture alliance (cra); WENN Rights Ltd (clb); Reuters Photographer (tr).
78–79 Alamy Stock Photo: Reuters/Alexandra Beier (r). **80 Alamy Stock Photo:** Alan Edward (clb). **Getty Images:** RAUL ARBOLEDA/AFP (crb). **80–81 RZSS:** (tc).
81 Dreamstime.com: Andrii Oliinyk (cr); Alexander Pokusay (tr). **Reid Park Zoo:** (br).
Shutterstock.com: Kirsty Wigglesworth/AP (bl). **82 Alamy Stock Photo:** Mark Waugh (br). **SEA LIFE Kelly Tarlton's Aquarium:** (tl).
82–83 SEA LIFE Kelly Tarlton's Aquarium: (tc). **83 Blue Planet Aquarium:** Roisin Maddison (bl). **SEA LIFE Kelly Tarlton's Aquarium:** (tr). **84–85 BluePlanetArchive.com:** Jeff Rotman. **84 Alamy Stock Photo:** Oleksii Bernaz (bc). **Precision Behavior:** A. Millwood-Lacinak (cl). **86–87 Getty Images:** Suhaimi Abdullah. **86 São Paulo Aquarium:** (bl). **uShaka Sea World:** (cl). **88 Alamy Stock Photo:** Arterra Picture Library (cl).
Two Oceans Aquarium: (clb).
88–89 Horniman Museum Aquarium: (c).
89 BluePlanetArchive.com: David Wrobel (crb). **Horniman Museum Aquarium:** (cra).
90 Alamy Stock Photo: Hannu Mononen (cra); WireStock (tc). **Getty Images/iStock:** MiryalaShop (cl). **Wildlife Reserves Singapore:** (br). **91 Alamy Stock Photo:** Friedrich von Hörsten (bc). **Aussie Ark:** (tr).
Reptilia Zoo: Ariana Emami (tl).
92–93 naturepl.com: Roland Seitre.
92 Shutterstock.com: Morphart Creation (tc). **93 naturepl.com:** Roland Seitre (tc, tc/taipan, tr). **94–95 Longleat Safari Park:** Ian Turner. **94 Getty Images:** Ajay Verma/Barcroft India (cl). **Tierpark Hellabrunn:** Marc Müller (bl). **96 123RF.com:** andreyoleynik (cr). **naturepl.com:** Nick Upton/2020VISION (cla, cl, clb).
96–97 naturepl.com: Roland Seitre (b).
97 Getty Images: Anadolu Agency/Omar Marques (cla). **98 Getty Images:** Arterra/Universal Images Group (cl). **98–99 Dublin Zoo:** Patrick Bolger (c). **99 Alamy Stock Photo:** Hemis (cb). **Pairi Daiza Zoo:** Pascale Jones (tr). **100 Alamy Stock Photo:** PA Images/Matt Crossick (bl). **100–101 Alamy Stock Photo:** PA Images/Tim Ireland.
101 Shutterstock.com: EPA/Bea Kallos (cla).
102 Smithsonian's National Zoo: (cl); Abby Wood (bl). **102–103 Alamy Stock Photo:** dpa picture alliance. **104 Chester Zoo:** (tl, cl, bl).
Shutterstock.com: Morphart Creation (fcr); Hein Nouwens (cr). **104–105 123RF.com:** fotointeractiva. **106–107 Getty Images:** Markus Scholz (l). **107 Alamy Stock Photo:** London Entertainment (crb). **108 Getty Images:** Anadolu Agency/Ray Tang (r).
109 Dreamstime.com: Channarong Pherngjanda (cl). **Getty Images:** AFP/Chris J Ratcliffe (cb); Oli Scarff (t); AFP/Daniel Leal-Olivas (cb/monkeys); NurPhoto/Wlktor Szymanowicz (crb). **110–111 Alamy Stock Photo:** PA Images/Joe Giddens (l).
111 Alamy Stock Photo: Guy Corbishley (crb). **Shutterstock.com:** Artur Balytskyi (cr). **112–113 Alamy Stock Photo:** ZUMA Press Inc (t). **112 Getty Images:** AFP/Roslan Rahman (crb). **113 Alamy Stock Photo:** Olaf Doering (bl). **114 Getty Images:** AFP/Tiziana Fabi (clb). **114–115 Science Photo Library:** Pascal Goetgheluck (c). **115 Alamy Stock Photo:** dpa picture alliance (cr, crb); mauritius images GmbH/Oliver Borchert (cra). **116 Dreamstime.com:** Andy Heyward (bc). **Getty Images:** Gallo Images/Sharon Seretlo (cl). **116–117 Getty Images:** Gallo Images/Sharon Seretlo (tr). **117 Getty Images:** Gallo Images/Sharon Seretlo (bl).
118–119 Getty Images: Marius Becker/DPA/AFP. **119 Alamy Stock Photo:** Arterra Picture Library (cb). **120 Alamy Stock Photo:** Joshua Hawley (bc); Andrey Khrobostov (cb).
120–121 Alamy Stock Photo: Michiel De Prins (c). **121 FUTUREMAG - ARTE:** (cra).
Getty Images: Bloomberg/Christophe Morin (cr, crb). **123 Getty Images/iStock:** Andrii-Oliinyk (c). **124–125 naturepl.com:** Jen Guyton (t). **124 RZSS:** (br). **125 Chester Zoo:** (bl). **126–127 Smithsonian's National Zoo:** (c). **126 Dorling Kindersley:** Dreamstime.com:Isselee (tl). **127 Alamy Stock Photo:** ZUMA Press, Inc. (br). **RZSS:** Gareth Bennett (tr). **Shutterstock.com:** I Made Dana (tl). **128 Getty Images/iStock:** Pimpay (cb). **(C) 2008 IUCN Red List Logo:** (bc). **128–129 Getty Images/iStock:** Phototreat (r). **130–131 Dreamstime.com:** Nikolay Denisov (c). **130 Planckendael Zoo, Belgium:** (bl). **Shutterstock.com:** Andrey Oleynik (tr). **131 Alamy Stock Photo:** Minden Pictures (tl); Natural History Collection (tr). **naturepl.com:** ZSSD (tc).
Planckendael Zoo, Belgium: (bl).
132–133 Taronga Conservation Society Australia: Rick Stevens (c). **132 Taronga Conservation Society Australia:** Bobby-Jo Photography (bl, c); Shallon McReaddie (cl); Rick Stevens (bc). **133 Alamy Stock Photo:** John Morris (tr). **Taronga Conservation Society Australia:** Bobby-Jo Photography (cr). **134–135 naturepl.com:** Eric Baccega (r).
134 Dreamstime.com: Mirquurius (bc).
naturepl.com: Eric Baccega (cl, c, clb, cb).
136 Shutterstock.com: Marzolino (clb).
136–137 uShaka Sea World: (c).
137 uShaka Sea World: (cra, cr, crb).
138 Getty Images/iStock: Byronsdad (t).
Shutterstock.com: DAVID MARIUZ/EPA-EFE (bl). **Zoos Victoria:** (bc). **139 Shutterstock.com:** Evgeny Turaev (tc). **Zoos Victoria:** (b).
140 Alamy Stock Photo: Chon Kit Leong (cra); Minden Pictures (tr); Tom Uhlman (br); Jane Tregelles (cl). **Longleat Safari Park:** Jessica Munday/enjoytheadventure (clb).
141 Alamy Stock Photo: Genevieve Vallee (tl); Xinhua (clb). Depositphotos Inc: Roman_Yanushevsky (tr). **142 Alamy Stock Photo:** Morgan Trimble (bl). **142–143 Alamy Stock Photo:** Life on white. **143 RZSS:** (bc, br). **144 Alamy Stock Photo:** Antiqueimages (cb). **Getty Images/iStock:** ugniz (bl).
144–145 naturepl.com: Jen Guyton (r).
146 Selamatkan Yaki: Reyni Palohoen (bl).
146–147 Selamatkan Yaki: Andrew Walmsley (c). **147 Alamy Stock Photo:** BIOSPHOTO (br). **148–149 Zoo Berlin. 149 Shutterstock.com:** Evgeny Turaev (cr). **Zoo Berlin:** (cb).
150–151 Getty Images: Jim Watson/AFP (b).
151 Alamy Stock Photo: UPI/Alexis C. Glenn. (tl). **153 naturepl.com:** Emanuele Biggi (tl); Edwin Giesbers (bl, cr). **154 Alamy Stock Photo:** Reading Room 2020 (cb).
154–155 Alamy Stock Photo: Finnbarr Webster (c). **155 Getty Images:** AFP/Saul Loeb (cra). **Smithsonian's National Zoo:** (cr, crb)

For further information see:
www.dkimages.com.